Beneath the Silence

Written by: Trinity Lease

Illustrated by: Marlette Youngs

Edited by: Tony Held

Copyrights

Table of Contents

To the child I was,

to the person I became,

and to the soul I am still learning to love.

This is for you. We made it.

WARNING: PLEASE READ

Before you turn the page, I want to say this:

This book is not fiction. It's not a story I made up or a tale designed to entertain. It's my life—raw, real, and unfiltered.

Every chapter you read comes from lived experience. Some of it will make you laugh. Some of it will probably make you cry. And some parts? They may make you want to close the book and walk away. I understand that. I've wanted to walk away from my own story more times than I can count.

But I didn't.

I wrote this for the girl who thinks no one would believe her.

For the mom who's hanging on by a thread.

For the woman who keeps forgiving what feels unforgivable—just to survive another day.

I wrote it because I believe truth has power, and sharing it might help someone else feel less alone.

That said, **this book contains sensitive and potentially triggering content**, including:

- Child abuse

- Sexual assault

- Drug addiction

- Mental health struggles

- Domestic dysfunction

Please take care of yourself as you read. If you need to pause, breathe, or come back later, do that. There's no right or wrong way to hold someone else's truth.

To protect the privacy of others, I've changed names and locations. But **every event is real**. Nothing here has been added for drama. Life provided plenty of that on its own.

If you've lived through something similar—if you've felt broken, silenced, or shattered—I hope you find something in these pages that makes you feel seen.

Thank you for being here.

You're braver than you think.

— *Trin*

Built on Broken Promises

2000: A Shotgun Wedding and Steel Toed Boots

My parents had a shotgun wedding once she found out she was pregnant with me. They did the whole shebang in Las Vegas at some chapel when my mom was 18 and everything. The marriage didn't last very long, though. One day, when I was around six months old, he came home from work, wearing steel-toed boots, in a rage over only God knows what. As they argued, it quickly got physical, and it ended with him kicking her repeatedly with his boots until she couldn't get up. The next day, when he went back to work, my mom packed as much stuff as possible and took off with me before he got home to try and stop us. She ended up filing a police report, which got us a restraining order against him and initiated the divorce process. This pushed through a custody arrangement that included supervised visits every other weekend. We would go to a place called Positive Connections; my mom would drop me off, and I would start to play in a huge room full of toys while a Social Worker watched over me. He would need to pass a drug test before he was allowed in the room where I was. There were cameras in every inch of that place; there was no way he could do anything to me or try to take me, although he very rarely came to these scheduled visits. He showed up maybe a handful of times.

I moved around a lot, and during kindergarten and first grade, I went to the same elementary school as my half and step brothers. My dad would send Barbies, clothes, letters, or anything else to boost his image as a father to school with them since he was not able to see me outside of that facility. Every time he did this, we had to report it to the caseworker because it was a violation of the restraining order, and he was determined to find any way to get close to us. He would show up at places we were living and bang on the door or drive past at all hours of the day and night. During this time, he would write my mom letters. Which, when I read these in my teenage years, really showed bipolar tendencies. One part would be about him yearning for us—talking about how much he loved us and wanted his family back. The next one would be full of threats and full-on crazy. It felt like he was trying to prove a point more than he was actually trying to be in my life.

2005: Supervised Visits and Circus Peanuts

My great-grandparents had adopted my dad when he was three years old, and they spoiled him rotten. In a way, that's why they fought so hard for me—they felt a deep sense of ownership and responsibility. My grandpa had served in World War II and, like many from his generation, held a lot of racist beliefs. I was my dad's firstborn: a fully white little girl with golden blonde hair and green eyes. I was his world. Every time he picked me up for a visit, we had a little tradition—we'd go to Orton's gas station in his town, where he would buy me a Bug Juice and a bag of circus peanuts. My half-brother, on the other hand, was half Native American, and it was clear that rubbed my grandpa the wrong way. He was never openly mean, but you could feel the difference in how he treated us. Everything changed after my grandpa died in 2007.

After his death, the truth about my biological dad started to show. It became clear that he didn't care for me the way I thought he did—it had been my grandparents holding that relationship together all along. Without them, my dad barely made an effort. He and my grandparents used to call Child Protective Services on my mom constantly, making up lies about our home being filthy with cat pee and unsafe to live in. None of the reports were ever true, but they were determined to try and take me away, and my dad was petty enough to go along with it.

As time went on, the visits became fewer and farther between, and the phone calls slowly faded away. Whenever he did call, he would blame my mom, saying she wouldn't let me talk to him or see him—but that was never true. Eventually, he started a new family, and it was obvious: I wasn't important to him anymore.

Growing up like that changed me in ways I spent years figuring out. From the start, I learned that the people who are supposed to love you the most can sometimes be the ones who hurt you the worst. My dad's anger, the violence toward my mom, all the games he played—it made me cautious of trusting people. Even as a little kid, I knew not everyone had good intentions, and that sometimes you had to protect yourself, even from your own family.

Moving from place to place, dealing with supervised visits, feeling the tension every time a package or letter showed up, I learned to be on guard, to read a room, to know when something wasn't right. I got used to broken promises early. It hurts, but after a while, you start expecting it, and that changes how you see the world.

2016: Thanks for the Twenty, Bitch

During this time, my aunt Jade was deep into drugs—totally unpredictable and all over the place. I was grounded after failing a drug test earlier that month, so I was already in deep shit. Since I wasn't allowed to drive, I had let her borrow my minivan. It wasn't anything special—basically a rolling heap—but it ran and got me from point A to point B. After about a month, she returned it... kind of. She didn't say a word, just parked it in front of my mom's house and dipped.

Later that day, I went outside to grab something I'd left in the van. I had no idea I was about to walk into a horror scene. The entire dashboard was torn to shreds—plastic everywhere, wires exposed and hanging like spaghetti. I had no clue how she even managed to drive it back in that condition. It looked like someone tried to hotwire it with a chainsaw. In the middle of the disaster, I spotted a crumpled-up $20 bill in the center console. I texted her:

"Yo, wtf did you do to my van?? I found $20 and I'm keeping it."
Then I moved on with my day, annoyed but whatever—thanks to her for this mess.

Later that week, my friend Valerie drove us across the highway to A&W for lunch before an event at the elementary school. I had that $20 on me and thought nothing of it. Another friend of mine, Heather, happened to be working the register, and when I handed her the bill, she paused—gave me a weird look and pulled out the counterfeit pen. She marked it, then hesitated. Her face said it all. She ended up handing it back to me, clearly unsure what to do. I was *pissed*—not just embarrassed, but furious. My cracked-out aunt really gave me fake money. My friend ended up paying for my lunch, and we left. As we pulled away, I rolled down the window and chucked that fake-ass bill onto the road.

About ten minutes later, my friend messaged me:

"Hey, just wanted to let you know—my boss came in after you left and said I was supposed to keep the bill and call the cops..."

You've *got* to be kidding me.

Thankfully, she convinced her boss not to report it—but if the cops had come for me over that, I wouldn't have taken the fall. I would've thrown my aunt under the bus so fast, and even shown them where she lived. No way was I going down for that crackhead.

2018: The Truck and the Trade

Since Derek was never really around, we were never on good terms. He always had something negative or cruel to say about my mom, which didn't sit well with me. But he did have one thing I wanted—something that, even though it wasn't in great shape, held sentimental value: my great-grandpa's truck. Derek had inherited it after my great-grandpa passed. The truck had already been damaged—it had been backed into a building and caught on fire—so it wasn't totally salvageable. But I still wanted it, just for what it represented.

I talked to my mom about it. Since my biological dad had never really paid child support—he owed around $35,000—she said she would be willing to write it all off if he gave me the truck. You can only do a write-off like that once in the state of Minnesota, and I was almost 18. I really was offering him a clean slate—a chance to get a real job and have a fresh start.

When I brought it up to him, he looked me right in the eye and said, "Fuck you. You're not getting shit, you ungrateful bitch." I could've changed his whole life by having him give me that truck, but instead, he threw my request in my face like it was trash. That moment showed just how selfish and self-centered he was raised to be. As I got older, I began to see who he really was. He never did anything for anyone but himself, and it hurt.

There were a few times in my young adult life when I tried to mend our relationship. I thought maybe if I showed him I loved him and wanted him around, he would change—for me, for my kids. I knew he was using drugs, but my biggest rule was: don't bring that around my children. I didn't care what he did on his own time. He always did the same thing—he'd build me up for a while. He'd call just to ask about my day or week. He'd tell me he loved me, which didn't happen often when I was a kid, so it meant more to me as an adult. It caught me off guard because a lot of the time, it was him calling me—not the other way around. That had never been the case. It had always been me chasing after him, asking to see him, and only getting to a quarter of the time.

I remembered going through a box of my old kindergarten papers once—little drawings and messy crafts—and realizing almost all of them were about him. Notes about how much I missed my dad, how much I loved him, like I was trying to call out to him before I even had the words to understand why he wasn't there. Seeing those scribbled hearts and tear-stained letters reopened wounds I'd convinced myself were long healed. It felt like I was hurting my own inner child all over again, tearing open memories I'd buried under years of "I'm fine." For a brief moment, when he called and said he loved me, it felt like maybe he finally did—but that hope just dug me deeper into old pain I thought I'd moved past.

I remember one year—I had to be around 15—he called my mom at 10 a.m. just to talk to me on my birthday. I hadn't heard from him in months, but it was still nice. I was surprised he remembered that year.

2021: A Graduation, A Glimmer

In 2021, I graduated with my first college degree. He came to my graduation, which was at my mom's house, with my brother. That situation could've gone either way—my parents hated each other with a burning passion—but they were civil for me. I had never felt anything like that before. At 21 years old, I was seeing them in the same room for the first time ever.

He took pictures with me and my oldest son, Noah, who was two at the time. He even interacted with my father-in-law and played with all the kids. He brought me three autographed baseballs, a vintage baseball helmet, and an autographed wooden baseball bat (which, honestly, is still my favorite weapon in a time of need). Things went well for about six months. He even drove an hour to visit me in the town where I lived.

Then one fall morning, I woke up to a full-page text message from him, absolutely freaking out:

"I'm so fucking done with your brother I don't want to see him anymore he's a dumb fuck I'm so done trying to be a dad I'm

just some guy you talk to not aloud to go to your house but it's
kool I will never come to your house I'm leaving on the 15 and I
dont expect to see you either and I wont be coming back either
I gave everything to my friend Diego you and your brother dont
deserve anything from me or anything that was grams and
grandpas"

He sent that to me at 3:04 a.m. I read it at 6 a.m. when I got up for
work. How do you even respond to that? Being as short-fused as him, I
gave him a taste of his own medicine. He stopped talking to me for a
while. Even though I was pregnant and hormonal, I was still hurt.

I sent him the Facebook link for my wedding event since we had
moved up the date and shortened the guest list. I knew deep down he
wouldn't show, but I still held onto that last shred of hope. Even amid all
the little things going wrong at my wedding, I noticed his absence. I had
other things to focus on, so I left it alone.

A month later, I started a job as a Housing Aide. I reached out to him:

"Hi. I started working at a new job I think can help you—it's the
Community Uplift Program in Rivermark. They help with
housing, including rent assistance for a whole year, especially

since you're homeless. Employment, child support issues, driver's license—everything. We have a program called Community Connect that I think you'd benefit from a lot. They have coordinators that can help with everything. Give me a call if you're interested. If not, I hope it's all going good for you. God gave me this job to help people, so that's why I'm reaching out."

I left it at that, hoping he'd come out of the woodwork and want to turn his life around. But the next time I checked, he had blocked me. I didn't hear from him for years, though I always heard the things he said about me and my mom. It's not easy to keep secrets when everyone in the county knows your family. The following year, he started hanging out with my aunt Jade's baby daddy, who was using at the time but still popped in and out of her place. He told Jack that he just dated my mom for a little while and that the only kid he had was Derek Jr.

Jack asked him, "I thought you were married to Deliah? And don't you have a daughter?"

He got real quiet.

Which made his words louder.

The Weight of Survival

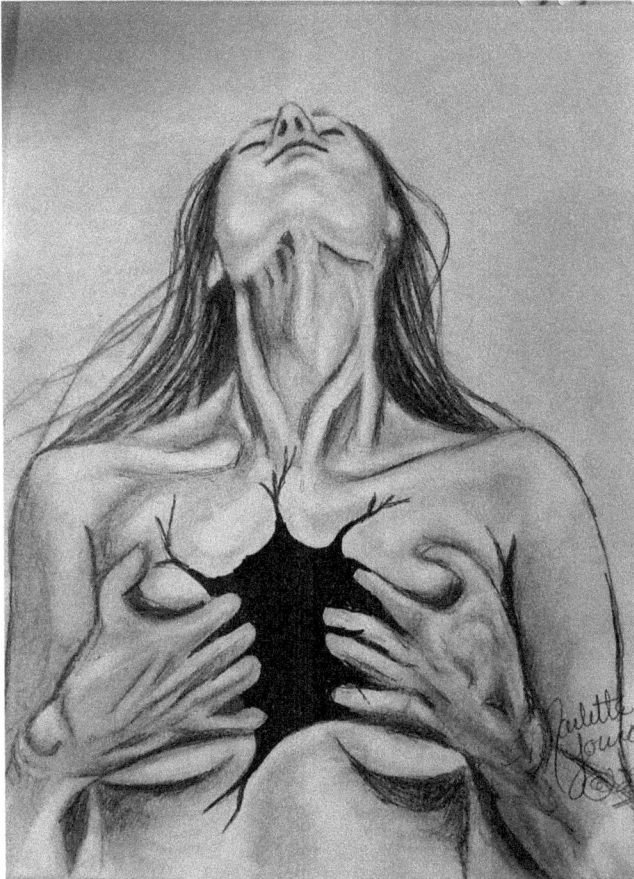

2007: When Blood Came Before Bedtime

It was a casual spring day for a seven-year-old, and her two-year-old baby sister—but what did I know? Mega Bloks, Barbie, and a tag along with the flowering of a growing vocabulary. Our mother and her new boyfriend, Calvin, had a tendency for strong language. Alex was such a kindhearted child that resembled a Cabbage Patch doll. From a young age, she was advanced when it came to growing her vocabulary compared to an average two-year-old. She was like a flame to paper, instantaneously absorbing all the new information. The room was filled with the laughter of our little voices as we had been running after Grandma Lenora's poodle through the living room the last five minutes or so. Without rhyme or reason, the word "shit" came tumbling from her mouth, because we had heard it enough from people around us. In a split second, Calvin whipped around, slapping her across the mouth with hands the size of her entire face.

Tears and screams echoed within the trailer home as blood ran from my sister's nose before anyone had time to react. Why would a mother allow her children to be exposed to these types of experiences?

That same year, they were married after the birth of my next sister, Lila. The first red flag should have been during a traffic stop earlier that year. Calvin had an active warrant for aggravated burglary and assault which were from prior to meeting my mom. During the stop, he tried to use his older brother Craig's ID to avoid arrest.

Craig was actually incarcerated at Moose Lake Correctional Facility for multiple DUI's, where he sat three out of a seven-year sentence already. By the end of his sentence, the State of Minnesota made him sit an extra two years on an involuntary commitment for being psychologically distressed while being a safety concern to himself and others, although I had never seen an ounce of violence from him. Calvin was caught in his lie after the officer asked Calvin's son, Mikey, who was seven at the time, what his dad's name was. Within the next ten minutes, there was my mom and two kids, in the back seat of the cop car.

Since I was so young, Calvin made me feel like I was in a scary movie, where it starts off good, then one by one each kid would disappear. Increasing the fear with each scene, there were times where he would be charming and say something to convince me the horror was over. Unfortunately for me, the carousel never stops turning.

Control, by the Blade

For a short time after Lila was born, we still lived with my grandma in her small trailer, tucked away in the middle of nowhere. I was just over seven years old, a little girl with long, curly, dirty blonde hair cascading down my back. At that age, I didn't yet understand how to care for my own hair. Without guidance or help it would easily tangle and mat overnight. No matter what I did, it never seemed to be enough. I wasn't neglectful on purpose--I was just a child. But that didn't stop the scolding. "You need to fucking take better care of your hair!" Calvin yelled. "It's a rat's nest." I hated these moments, the way my stomach would tighten with shame. My hair had a mind of its own, wild and untamed. No matter how much I tried, I couldn't seem to make it behave the way they wanted.

One Sunday morning, as I sat at the kitchen table with my sisters, perched on our Snow White bench, Calvin walked in. He took one look at me and shook his head disgustedly. "I'm tired of looking at you like this, " he said, his voice sharp. "If you can't take care of it, you don't get to have it." Before I could react, he grabbed a chair and dragged it to the middle of the kitchen with a screech. My heart pounded as he yanked open the knife drawer and pulled out a dull pair of kitchen scissors. I didn't move. I didn't breathe.

He grabbed me out of my seat with a tight grasp on my upper arm and threw me into the chair. Without hesitation, he started chopping. The dull blades snagged and tugged at my scalp as he hacked away at my curls. He had no idea what he was doing--no plan, no care, just fury and impatience. Strands of my hair fell to the floor, landing in uneven piles around me. He kept cutting and cutting until my once-long hair was above my ears, butchered and uneven. The curls made it look even shorter, the choppy cuts leaving gaps where my hair should have framed my face. His goal wasn't just to cut my hair. His goal was humiliation. He wanted me to be embarrassed when I walked out of that trailer, to feel the sting of shame when I went to school, to make sure everyone saw what I had lost. And I did, I felt it. The loss, the humiliation, the powerlessness.

2008: The Price of a Wrong Turn

We had moved around a lot, almost every year, but sometimes more. My twin brothers were born in 2008 and we had lived in a little green house in Foxview. We were only a couple blocks from the elementary school, so there was no bus to pick me up. I had to walk to school every day, and on the first day of third grade I got lost for over an hour trying to find my way home. As a very independent eight-year-old I did not want to look like I didn't know where I was going. I was pretty sure I knew where I was going, but I was wrong. I set off walking in the complete opposite direction, trying to find something that looked familiar to get me home. I walked half a mile before my cousin came by on her bike and found me. I ended up somewhere by the water treatment plant, just a bunch of metal domes in a fenced area. She didn't have pegs or any way for me to sit on her bike frame but between her handlebars and her seat. The ride home hurt so bad, because I had a big piece of metal up my butt. I definitely got scolded once I made it home, for worrying everyone. I made a friend in my grade who lived close by so I would walk to her house in the morning and then we would walk the rest of the way to school together. This kept me from getting lost again.

There was a spring afternoon when my walking buddy stayed home sick. The neighbors right next to us had two dogs who were usually really nice and on leads since their yard was not fenced. I waved at the dogs as I passed by, but when I was about halfway past, I noticed one of the dogs wasn't on the lead and it was running towards me. Fear hit me immediately, and I started sprinting home with the dog getting closer and closer. The faster I ran, the faster he ran, and then he caught up to me. He bit me right in my butt cheek, breaking skin and bruising almost instantly. I ran into the house, tears pouring down my face. I face-planted into the couch right next to where my mom was sitting. She was confused and started to panic, and I was hyperventilating so much I could barely tell her what happened, besides holding my butt and screaming. Once we walked into the bathroom, she pulled down my pants and saw the damage. She worked to calm me down the best she could while Calvin went next door to talk to the neighbor. I'm not sure how that conversation went, but I did not see those dogs off the lead again while we lived there. Nevertheless, I was so terrified that every day walking to and from school the rest of the year, I took the extra long way.

2011: The Silent Burn

We moved into an old farmhouse 27 miles outside town a few months earlier. It was surrounded by trees and cornfields. We rented it from a diabetic farmer who had recently become wheelchair-bound after losing a leg to his diabetes. The longer we lived there, the more often we found used syringes hoarded and hidden across the property from the owner not properly disposing of them. At this time, I was 11 years old and the oldest of five siblings: two sisters aged five and six, and twin brothers aged three. After my twin brothers were born, our mom started bouncing between two jobs that changed with each move throughout the years.

With my mom being absent 90% of the time due to odd split shifts, and the need for sleep, it gave Calvin all the power. There was no one there to tell him otherwise, as if he would listen anyway. Calvin had a few odd-end jobs primarily in manual labor and manufacturing that he never held more than a week or two, where he walked off in anger and never returned. We had a tan pit bull named Brandi who got knocked up by a stray during her first heat and ended up with eight puppies. We recently had got Brandi; she was barely over a year old. Shortly after having her litter, Calvin would lock her outside, separated from her babies, for hours in below-zero weather. Her health declined quickly, likely due to how unsanitary her environment was during birth. She was stuck in a large wire kennel in the corner of the living room. Inside were old raggedy towels that smelled of urine and feces.

Off to school, I went on what seemed like a normal winter Monday. When I returned home after my two-hour bus ride, I reached for the door to go inside. The once golden doorknob was now dented, covered in scratches and blood. You could see the indents of her teeth and scratch marks covering half the bottom of the door. You could tell this kind of damage had to have been done over several hours of her fighting to get inside to her babies. Brandi was nowhere in sight. Adrenaline rushed through my body as I ran into the empty house, searching for her in a panic. Back outside, I screamed her name for what felt like days. My voice became hoarse, and tears flowed from my eyes.

Hours later, my family pulled into the driveway after being gone. God knows where and for how long, since Alex and I were the only school-aged kids out of five. Calvin stepped out of the truck and walked over near where I was sitting. He paced for a moment pretending to look for even a trace of Brandi. Moments passed, and then he said, "You know she was really sick; she honestly probably went to find somewhere to die."

His voice was as cold as the air around us. He then turned and went inside following my mother and siblings as if he hadn't just stomped on my heart. Alex was the only one old enough to know something was up. After this, we all went on as if nothing had happened, I mean we had eight puppies to get rid of. I went straight to my room to thaw the tears on my cheeks.

During our stay here, we discovered many stray kittens around the property, including a very sweet gray kitten who spent most of its time trying to get inside, away from the cold. Calvin hated cats with a burning passion, though he never did say why. He always told us stories of pets he had over the years, one even being a skunk. After Brandi was gone, he put out bowls of antifreeze, hoping to poison the kittens. It made me wonder if he'd do the same to Brandi. As time went on, there were fewer kittens every day. But that gray kitten stuck it through until one day when Calvin approached me and offered me ten dollars to lure the kitten to an area so he could shoot it with an Airsoft gun until it died. Tears in my eyes, I did as he asked.

As the winter went on, Calvin actually was engaging and spending time with me. This was one of extremely few times during an 11-year period. I loved going on snowmobile rides, feeling the wind in my face. No matter how cold I got, it just hit different. One afternoon he said, "If you can start it, you can drive it." With hope and excitement in my face, I pulled the recoil and enjoyed the instant satisfaction of the rumble when it started. He was shocked and regretted telling me I could drive it. At first, he electrical taped a deck of playing cards under the throttle, to keep me from going too fast. I did laps around and around the house, out to the field and back again. After an hour or so, he removed the deck of cards. I kept doing laps, and as time went on I began to be careless. I went to take another round, but instead of pressing the brake to slow down around the corner, I accidentally floored the throttle. Within seconds everything went black.

I have no idea how much time passed before I woke up half leaned up against a tree with the snowmobile feet from me. It was still running, but the handlebars were bent. I remembered that he told me anytime I needed it to stop, to hit the kill switch. I crawled over and pressed the button, making it a lot quieter out there. My head was screaming, and I had blood running down my forehead. The plastic visor on the top of the helmet had broken and cut my face open. I was instantly terrified for my life. Calvin is going to kill me. Oh my god what have I done, what will happen to me... I managed to get up and hobble around the house. I started crying as I walked up to Calvin. I was hysterical. I repeated how sorry I was and that I broke his snowmobile. After all, I was 11 and had no idea of anything about snowmobiles up until an hour ago. He laughed it off assuming I was being dramatic. "Let's go take a look. I'm sure it's fine"

That gave me a sigh of relief. Once we got to the back where the totalled snowmobile was laying, his facial expression changed quickly. This is exactly what I feared. "Get your ass in the house!" he screamed at me. I turned and ran as fast as my body would let me , what with how sore I was feeling. I hid in my room the rest of the night until he calmed down a bit. That night felt like one of the scariest I'd ever had, but it wasn't the last time I felt that way. Just when I thought things were finally starting to settle down, something even worse happened.

We lived here for a while, maybe longer than some of the other places. The house was heated by a wood stove that was in the basement. Since I had never seen it, I didn't really think about it. One winter night I was woken up by being dragged out of my bed by my shirt. I hit the floor like dead weight and woke up instantly. I couldn't see a thing, and I could hardly breathe. But I did get a glimpse of the person who'd awakened me: my mom. Her face was full of fear, and mine probably was too. There was no escaping the smoke. It was everywhere. I tried not to breathe it in, but I couldn't help it. My lungs burned, my eyes stung, and my chest felt tight. It got harder to see, harder to breathe—harder to move. All I knew was that we had to get out. There was smoke everywhere, and my mom had one sister in her arms and pulled the other by the hand behind. We all managed to get out of the house to sit in the Suburban that was parked outside. The entire house was engulfed in flames. Shortly after we had three fire departments show up and take an hour or so to put out the fire. At 2 a.m. all of us were tired and scared. Even though it was the middle of the night, our yard was lit up like it was the day, the flames growing minute by minute. Since we lived 40 minutes outside town, it took roughly 30 minutes or so for three different fire departments to arrive, with a total of six fire trucks filling the yard. We sat for a while watching the burning wreckage, then we headed to my grandma's to get some sleep. Once everything was aired out and we were allowed back in, Calvin had talked to the firemen about how it could've possibly happened. You can't burn any kind of wood in stoves like these. The wood used often was pine, which usually had a lot of sap. The sap ended up collecting in the chimney until it was enough to start a fire. Careless on his part.

2012: The Bet that Hurt

There were a few years that we lived in this house, and we were trying to buy it with a contract for deed instead of a standard mortgage because it was not like we had the income documentation for that. Most of our money was under the table. Since all of my other siblings were pretty young, and we had a dog, they were going to put up a privacy fence. They didn't make it past a few panels and posts for several weeks. Calvin had a friend named Chadifer who brought over a mini dirt bike. Just the right size for me. Calvin and his friend really wanted to see me drive it, and they made bets on me.

Once I got on the bike, I was very unsteady, thankful I could touch the ground. I struggled to go around the garage and find my footing. I hit the throttle a little too hard and went flying forward towards the fence. There was a lone post in a random spot, and I hit it dead on. After that I flew through the air, skidding on the gravel for a foot or two. Blood running from my eye, I started crying. He came running over to me, since they just watched it happen. He stood me up, dusted off the dirt and said,

"You're fine! You didn't even hit the ground that hard." So not only was I hurt, he pointed out that my feelings didn't matter.

You know what's crazy? I had a red scar on my face for over 8 years after that.

2013: The Flood of Control

It was a typical summer day, the kind where the sun blazed overhead and the air smelled of warm grass and wet pavement. My siblings and I were playing in the sprinklers, running through the cool spray, laughing as the water droplets caught the sunlight. It was supposed to be fun. Then Calvin grabbed the hose.

At first it seemed like he was joining in, spraying each of us directly, turning the game into roughhousing. But there was something more aggressive, more forceful. I could see it in his face, the way his jaw tightened, the way his eyes darkened. Panic surged through me. Water had always been something that terrified me. Ever since I was a toddler, I nearly drowned more than once. That fear had lived inside of me, deep and unshakable. It didn't take much, just the sight of water rushing toward me in a way I couldn't control, for that fear to tighten around my chest.

The yard stretched wide around us, two full lots with two driveways, the remnants of a freshly torn down cabin scattered nearby, and a flimsy metal swing set that was passed down through several families which stood rusting in the corner. Off to the side was our so-called "playhouse," a small structure pieced together from old pressed boards, barely holding together. It had a makeshift doorway, a single window, and a skylight that let in slivers of sunlight. I ran. It didn't think--I just bolted across the yard, sprinting away from a grown man whose face twisted with rage. Just seconds ago it had been a game. Now it wasn't. How could someone flip a switch so fast?

I ran nearly 400 feet, my heart pounding, straight to the playhouse, my only hope of escape. I ducked inside, pressing myself into the corner, trying to disappear. Maybe if I stayed still, if I made myself small enough, he would stop. Maybe he would just walk away. But Calvin didn't stop. By the time he reached me, he was holding the hose with both hands, knuckles white. He didn't hesitate. He lifted the hose over the skylight, aiming the high pressure stream straight down. Then he turned it on.

The force of the water hit me like a punch, knocking the breath from my lungs. It filled my nose, my mouth–I couldn't breathe, couldn't scream. It didn't stop. The water kept coming relentlessly, drowning me where I sat. I thrashed, gasping for air, but there was nowhere else to go. The playhouse wasn't a safe haven--it was a trap. From a distance my siblings watched, too afraid to do anything, too afraid to even move. They knew what I knew. There was no stopping him.

The Wounds We Carry

Social media platforms like Facebook, Twitter, and Snapchat were becoming increasingly popular. With Calvin's controlling nature, I wasn't allowed to engage on these platforms. I spent time at the library with my sister, sneaking onto the desktop computer to fit in with my eighth grade classmates who had social media. One day, after riding my bike over a mile home, my mom told me my older cousin had seen my Twitter account. She wasn't angry, but she warned me to delete it to avoid Calvin's wrath. My mom was too tolerant of his behavior. She had five kids now, after all, and she refused to be a single mom again. I was never told if she was scared of him or not, but how could she not be?

That night, Calvin came upstairs yelling. I immediately went to my room. Not long after, I heard glass shatter, followed by my mother's screams. I ran upstairs to find blood trailing from her room into the kitchen where large knives were scattered amongst the mess. I came to find out that during the altercation, my mom was fed up and threatened to leave him. At some point, he attempted to punch my mom, but she moved too quickly, and he shattered the mirror closet doors.

Calvin was outside, obviously in a mental health crisis, revving his truck engine, trying to destroy my mom's only means of transportation. A rush of terror-fueled energy took over my body, and I screamed, "That's real mature!" Which was a real ballsy move if you ask me. I just jumped when I saw bloody handprints covering my mom's back, unknowing whose blood it really was.

Before I could comprehend, he slammed his truck into park and had already made it the short distance to the house, where my mom held him at the door with all her weight. Down the stairs I went to snatch up my phone, the kind that takes three buttons for one letter in a text message. I maneuvered my way down a narrow, moist crawl space and hid behind the water softener, where Calvin could not get to me. I called 911. I was shaky and clammy, trying to tell the operator what happened. In less than ten minutes, several police cars surrounded the house like you would see in a movie. I stayed on the phone silently as I peeked out of the space until the police stormed down the stairs to take him into custody.

It being a weekend, he only sat a few days, and my mom did not let him come home for several weeks. He was charged with domestic violence in addition to court ordered anger management classes, outpatient treatment, Alcoholics' Anonymous meetings, and supervised probation to which he did not ever comply. His probation officer was so unconcerned, it took her two years to issue a warrant, when he was on his deathbed, and it was too late. He was never held responsible for the things he did that were burned into my brain. Is this the worst I'd see? Could it get better?

2014: Memories in the Dark

Living in an unfinished basement had its perks. All my younger siblings were upstairs, and Calvin would have to come all the way downstairs to torment me. I had one purple fuzzy rug on a bare concrete floor. When the lights were off, only a shred of light came through the hopper window under the steps going outside. The strangest things happened in that room. My room was directly under the sliding door to the backyard. There was a day where as a typical 14-year-old, I liked sleeping in when I could, which wasn't often with having four younger siblings to take care of.

SLAM! Down came my lamp and all the bulbs shattered. It was one of those with six flexible lights, all with different color shades. I was nervous to go upstairs because obviously someone was so upset to slam the door above so hard for it to rattle the wall and knock down my lamp. I waited and listened for any other commotion, but there was none. I checked my phone and it was only 10:17 a.m. I crept my way up the stairs with caution. The faint sound of cartoons on the TV came from the living room, and Calvin was sitting at the kitchen table enjoying a cup of coffee. I was confused. I came up to the table and asked, "Did you slam the door a little bit ago?" He looked at me like I was crazy. "No?" he replied. I explained what happened with my lamp and was wondering how it happened. No one had moved in a couple hours.

I shrugged it off like nothing and went along with my day. Later that day, my friend Jennifer came over to hang out, which was happening slim to none. We ended up hiding out in my room to avoid the annoying little siblings I had upstairs. For some reason we decided we wanted to play hide and seek in the dark, even though there was, like, no space. Since my room was pitch dark with the lights off, it was the perfect space for this. I was sitting on my bed and Jennifer went over to the wall about 7 feet from there to turn off the light. I stood up and, boom, down I went. Jennifer turned the light on because I tripped over something, but there was nothing there. Maybe something tripped me. Now here I was with a set of braces imprinted on my forehead from when I fell into her.

Even now, I'm not sure what to make of that day—whether it was just a string of weird coincidences or something else entirely. But what I do know is that living in that basement taught me to trust my gut and to stay alert in spaces that didn't always feel safe, even if nothing could be seen. It's strange how certain memories stay sharp, like the sound of shattered glass or the echo of silence that follows something unexplainable. That basement held more than just my bed and a purple fuzzy rug—it held a version of me learning to navigate fear, loneliness, and resilience, one strange moment at a time.

We moved a couple more times before finding a house that had enough rooms for all of us; I even had my own. Since I had never known what it was like to be treated normally by a man, the experiences I sought out were not like those of other kids my age.

2016: Under the Street Light

That year was some of my lowest times in my childhood. Sure a good thing would happen sometimes, but I went through a lot during that time. Honestly, it seemed like the world was crumbling around me. There was a six-month period where it was pure chaos, like it was a weird version of *The Purge,* but real. There was a skyrocket in killer clown sightings and attacks from August till November all over the United States and 18 other countries. There was a case in Pennsylvania where a teenage boy was stabbed 27 times by a clown. They would target areas like schools, rural cities, wooded areas, or other areas that had a limited police presence.

I hadn't heard about anything in my area, so when I would sneak out a lot, I never considered the risk. I had a couple friends in their late 20s that lived in the trailer court a couple blocks over. Mainly go hang out, smoke some weed, then head home to get a few hours of sleep before school. It was about 2 a.m. and I was headed for home. With limited street lights, it gave a wary vibe. My vision is pretty bad, even with my glasses, especially things far away. A couple blocks down, maybe 600 feet from where I was standing, I saw a figure directly under one of the few street lights. Panic surged through me, and I swore it was one of those killer clowns, but I had a second guess. Until I saw him start running towards me. I started sprinting for home, as fast as my feet could carry me. I was a smoker, so my lungs were not very happy with me.

I scrambled into the house not caring to be quiet, slammed the door closed and locked both locks, and then I slid down the door and sat on the floor to catch my breath. The door to the porch didn't lock, only the house door, so a few minutes after I got inside, I heard the wooden door creak open. I was below the window of the door and the house was dark. I could hear his footsteps and the sound of him trying to open the door, slamming his shoulder into it. I did not move a muscle. Until I heard him leave, I waited, then slowly peeked out every window in the house making sure he was gone.

I'd become a magnet for chaos and terror, as if Calvin had an endless supply of schemes designed purely to push me over the edge.

Searching for Love in the Wrong Places

I made it through day by day, with no idea what was to come. Calvin was admitted to the hospital in Rivermark often, undergoing many surgeries for bowel obstructions over six months. It did make my life a bit calmer because, with him gone, there was no one to shove me to the ground, throw things at me like lamps, dishes, or whatever was within an arm's reach from across the room, or degrade my self worth each time he had the chance. I could just breathe for a minute.

By this time in my life, I had started calling him Dad. I visited him every chance I got and told him about my day and my friends, as if he had never broken me down to nothing, with the hope that he would treat me the way a father should. I was in turmoil, confused and scared about what would happen to him. His surgeries were not helping. By November, he was diagnosed with terminal lymphatic cancer. Everyone tried to keep us from knowing what was going on, to the point me and my siblings stayed at my grandparents' place while my mom and grandma tended to Calvin's hospice care at our home, but between Stockholm syndrome and idolizing him, I pushed my way in. I watched him physically disintegrate before my eyes. Not only was the cancer attacking his organs, he was also dropping weight extremely fast. He was probably around 170 pounds, and within 60 days, he was maybe a hundred pounds soaking wet.

By this time, he could not take his pills orally and required IV pain medications. This became my "in." He had bottles and bottles of oxycodone and morphine; he could barely see, so how was he going to know if I took a few? The need to fill the void grew stronger with the depression. I was without a mother to confide in, because she shut down any sensitive topic. She did not have to say it; we simply did not talk about things like that. Self-medicating was a regular occurrence for me that maximized overtime.

The euphoric rush was the reason to chase the high. A few turned into a few more and then a full bottle. I would usually visit him after school and tell him about my day, even when I was not sure he could hear me. I was talking to him a week before he died when he tried to push me away with the little strength he had, hoarsely screaming at me to get out over and over. I ran from the room to my mom and grandma in the kitchen, where my mom held me like a little kid while I cried. A week later I was at school, scrolling through Facebook during health class, when I saw my uncle had posted, "RIP to my brother Calvin" two hours earlier. I managed to get on the bus before the tears started rolling.

When I got to my grandma's, I went straight to the spare room in the basement and cried for hours. I do not know if it was the trauma he caused me, or the hero I made him out to be during his illness, but I do think he is the reason that sparked my addiction. My grandpa came down because I had not even checked in when I got home. He knew I knew and just let me be. How shitty was it for me to find that out on social media? I was not pulled from school or called. Why was I not included? I was sixteen; I had watched him shrivel up over the past six months. What did I do to deserve this?

Gravel & Grace

What a year it had already been—we were just surviving, taking it one day at a time. Even though Calvin was gone, some of his friends still lingered. His crew was made up of troublemakers—crackheads, really—who constantly got themselves into messes, always pushing the limits. It was Thanksgiving Day. We had gone across town to my grandma Lenora's house, which was packed wall to wall with family. Aunts, uncles, cousins, siblings—you name it. At least 40 people crammed into her small rambler. We were all waiting for my uncle Kent, who was supposed to pick up Clay and his girlfriend and bring them to dinner.

But time kept passing, and he still hadn't shown up. My mom finally decided to call him. She glanced over at me, covered her ears against the noise, and stepped outside. It felt... off. When she came back in, though, she acted like everything was fine. We started getting everyone ready to sit down for grace. Less than five minutes later, three Grey Birch County sheriff's deputies burst through the front door—guns drawn. Panic hit the room like a wave. Everyone standing near the entry scattered. My grandma fought her way through the crowd, pushing toward the officers.

"What are you doing?!" she yelled. "This is my family—it's Thanksgiving!"

They were looking for Clay. No one knew why. I had never seen my grandma that upset. The cops searched the entire packed house, then left about ten minutes later, leaving my grandma in tears. My mom gave me a side glance and jerked her head toward the front door. I followed her out without a word. Whatever was going on, it wasn't good. We tore through back streets and screeched into our driveway. She slammed the truck into park before it had even stopped, and we both jumped out. We slipped through the gate and into the house through the back door. It was eerily quiet.

Then I noticed it—random $20 bills lying under the table, near the walls. The laundry room looked like it had been turned upside down, and the bathroom door was closed. Something was definitely wrong. We walked through and stopped. The rug near the crawl space door was crooked and half-stuck—definitely not how we left it.

The tension was suffocating.

We closed the door behind us, then heaved open the heavy hatch to the crawl space. And there they were—Clay and his girlfriend, crouched in the gravel below, fear written all over their faces. We didn't say a word. We just shut the hatch and carefully repositioned the rug. We picked up the scattered bills, tidied up the house like nothing had happened, got back in the truck, locked the doors, and headed back to grandma's to help settle the chaos.

Later, after the kids were distracted and some of the family had left, a group of us gathered outside with my uncle and some of the other adults, smoking and decompressing. Uncle Kent told us what happened. He'd gotten pulled over on the way with Clay and his girlfriend. The cops questioned them about some stolen ATMs in Maple Hollow. Kent said they were just on their way to Thanksgiving dinner. The police took impressions of all their shoes and let them go. But they weren't far from Clearwater Ridge, and they knew the cops would be coming once the footprints were matched. So they sped down the highway, dropped Clay and his girlfriend off behind my house in a back alley, and Kent returned to grandma's like nothing was wrong. When we got home later that night,they were gone. But the money wasn't.

Now, I know this might sound like just another selfish crackhead doing dumb things. But Clay was different. Out of all Calvin's friends, I had never met anyone like him. He saved me more times than I can count. When Calvin would get aggressive, Clay was the one who stepped in and made him back down. He was my best friend. My hero. He spent years bouncing around the U.S. before ending up in prison in Arizona for something stupid. But honestly, maybe that's what he needed. He came out the same Clay—but with a better vision for what he wanted in life.

I can never thank him enough.

Boys & Men

2012: Where Childhood Ends

We lived in a town called Birchfield for about 1.5-2 years, where we made friends with a family down the street. Their dad worked with my mom at the turkey egg packaging plant for a while. They were a very odd family and they had three sons. One was my age, the second was two years older, and the oldest was a senior in high school. We spent a lot of time there, especially after their mom started babysitting my twin baby brothers and my little sister for my mom so she could work.

During the summer, they had an above ground pool that we all swam in. All day, every day. Along with a trampoline to jump on. One day we all got wild hair and decided to take a ladder to climb on top of the shed and dive into the pool. We started off by being careful not to slip and fall, but as the day went on we got a little more ballsy. One out of a hundred times that I did this, I lost my footing and fell backwards off the shed to the ground. I was full of adrenaline and I felt okay, so I climbed back up right away and jumped in. Oh my god, my legs were on fire. I got out of the pool as quickly as I could to sit on the trampoline to figure out what was going on. As I looked down, I saw blood pouring down both my legs. I started to panic at the sight of it, and began crying uncontrollably.

Their mom came rushing over with towels, trying to wrap her head around what just happened. We found a roll of rusty barbed wire under the ladder where I fell. My parents weren't home, so once I was calm I hobbled my way down the street with dried blood on both legs to clean myself up at home. I took such a long shower to get the bleach out of each fine cut.

The more time we spent there, the more Logan, the eldest, creeped me out. He was always trying to be in my space, which eventually he did. He was weird and kind of nerdy. He had this big static electricity wand with a huge plastic bubble on top. Originally it started out that everyone would pile into his basement room in the pitch dark and play around with this wand that lit up the room, in an exciting way. As time went on each other kid who was usually there would drop out one by one until it was just me and Logan. A concrete floor with one small rectangle shag carpet rug, walls which had early 70s shiplap panelling from top to bottom, and a twin size bed on an unstable metal frame. As soon as the lights were off, there was no way out, not a shred of light to be seen. When I would sit on the edge of his bed, in the dark, a sudden rush of adrenaline would wash over me. I could not see anything or anyone. I flinched as Logan's cold, sweaty hands touched my leg. I could feel his large class ring on his finger as he moved his hand from my thigh up to my shoulders and slowly pushed me back to lay on his bed. Still pitch dark, then flash, the static wand lit up the room. Every time a point in the wand was touched, the static pattern would change. As he changed it over and over, he waved it in front of me as if he had me in a trance. As he moved his hands up my shirt or down my pants, my body froze. All I could hear was my heartbeat in my ears. Suddenly his 12-year-old brother busted through the door and flipped the light on, as any other younger brother would do, because what is privacy when you're that age. I felt a sigh of release as I jumped up and ran out the room.

Looking back, my time in Birchfield was a strange mix of innocence and violation. There were carefree summer days full of laughter, scraped knees, and childhood adventures—but also moments that forced me to grow up far too quickly. At the time, I didn't have the words or understanding to name what was happening in that dark basement, but I knew something about it felt deeply wrong. Now, with the clarity that comes with age, I see those experiences for what they were. They shaped how I understand trust, safety, and boundaries. Even though that chapter of my life holds both joy and trauma, I carry it with me—not as a weight, but as a reminder of how far I've come.

2014: Porch Weed & Short Stack

The few friends I had back then were mostly stoners. I didn't really go anywhere except the park or the gas station, but one afternoon, I got a wild idea. Ty, a kid who lived in the blue apartments a couple of blocks from my mom's house, invited me over. It was a summer day during the week, and it was just me, Ty, and Nico—who, by the way, was a weird 30-year-old hanging out with a 16-year-old and a 14-year-old. We raided Ty's mom's wine fridge, and between the three of us, we drank four bottles of wine. We were definitely asking for trouble.

Later that evening, Nico invited me to a house party at a trailer court nearby. I was nervous, but Ty was with me, so I figured I'd be okay. But when we got there, everyone at the house was over 30—mostly guys—and I immediately became the center of attention. I hadn't even hit puberty yet, so there was nothing really exciting about me, but that didn't seem to stop them. Already a little drunk, the first thing we did was smoke weed on the front porch. I was standing near a pile of shoes when I got so high that I fell over, straight onto the ground, like a tree toppling over.

There was this older guy, maybe around 40, named Blake. He had

been flirting with me all night and got everyone to start calling me

"Short Stack." Eventually, he picked me up and carried me over to the

couch to lay down. After a while, everyone gathered in the living room,

turned on some old western movie, and started frying chicken. My

memory's fuzzy, but I do remember Nico sitting next to me, eating fried

chicken with grape jelly on it. Honestly, it was so good—though, I didn't

expect that combination. At some point, I got a little uncomfortable. I had

two grown men sitting really close to me on the couch, and I was dozing

in and out of sleep.

The next morning, I woke up with wild hair, half hanging off the

couch. There was an older lady asleep on the couch next to mine, and

three men were spread out on the floor around the couches. I checked my

phone and saw that Calvin had been blowing it up. My heart dropped. I

felt like garbage and had no energy to come up with a good excuse. I

tiptoed over the passed-out people, trying to find Ty, but he was nowhere

to be found. That bastard must have left at some point, leaving me there

with no idea what had happened. My bike was laying in the yard, so I

picked it up and started walking home. I was so hungover that riding it felt like it might make me puke. The walk wasn't far, but it gave me a chance to pull myself together.

When I walked in the door, Calvin was waiting. "Where have you been? You didn't come home or answer any of our calls!" he said, his voice sharp. I quickly responded, "I was with my friends, and we spent so much time outside yesterday that we must have fallen asleep early. I didn't hear my phone. I'm sorry." He seemed satisfied with that. "Okay, just try not to do that again." Phew. That was close. I promised myself I wouldn't make that mistake again. For about a year after that, Blake kept trying to message me on every social media platform, asking me to come to their parties or just hang out. Yeah, no thanks.

The Whisper of Broken Trust

In 2014, I started at Clearwater Ridge High School. It was my third school that year, and I was still only in eighth grade. With all the moving around, it was hard to feel like I belonged anywhere. Clearwater Ridge had this annual tradition called Day of Caring where students spent a day helping out in the community—yard work, cleaning, whatever was needed. Then in the afternoon, we could pick fun activities like karaoke, tie-dyeing, or watching movies. I usually gravitated toward the lunchroom, where the karaoke happened. I was too shy to sing, but I liked the energy. One time, an older boy sang "Boys 'Round Here" by Blake Shelton. He was loud, confident, and laughing with another guy about the chewing tobacco lyrics. I didn't know it yet, but that boy—Theo—would end up changing the course of my life.

The next school year, I started making more friends. Theo was often in our lunch group. We were also in choir together. He'd look at me during class, and I started looking back. We didn't seem like a likely match—him, a football player; me, the quirky new girl—but we connected. Quickly and intensely. We kept our relationship a secret. His mom was strict, and because of our age difference and the laws in our state, we knew it wouldn't be allowed. Still, I went to every football game I could, cheering for him in his #85 jersey. One day, after a game, he said his mom joked he must have a girlfriend. For a moment, we hoped she'd be okay with us. She wasn't. We were forced to break up.

Even after the breakup, we stayed in touch. We passed notes through lockers and friends. But then Theo had a mental health crisis—he tried to run away and ended up in a psychiatric hospital. I felt like I was falling apart. I was already battling my own depression, and his absence hit hard. To cope, I began self-harming—one cut for every day he was gone. By the time he came back, I had twenty-seven marks, some of which I'd reopened and deepened.

When he returned, we still couldn't be together publicly. But the secret notes continued. One day, he asked me to meet him in a back entryway of the school at 5:30 p.m. I snuck over, heart pounding. When I saw him, it felt like time froze. He hugged me tight, kissed my face and neck, and suddenly it all escalated. He pressed me against the wall, hands roaming. I was nervous—my past experiences with intimacy weren't good—and I didn't want to do anything in that open space. He suggested we move to the handicap stall in the boys' bathroom. I hesitated... but said yes. After that, things started to unravel.

Not long after we parted ways, Theo changed. The boy I once cared for started spreading rumors about me—*cruel* rumors. He told people I didn't know how to take care of myself, nicknaming me "The Jungle" because I hadn't learned about grooming. No one had ever taught me about feminine hygiene or sexual health. I only shaved my legs because I saw other girls doing it. Everything else was a mystery. And now it was being used against me. The nickname spread like wildfire. Boys from different grades started using it. The hallways filled with whispers, snickers, and humiliating comments. I felt stripped bare—exposed, ashamed, powerless.

Eventually, it began to quiet down. Theo was sent away again—more behavioral issues—and ended up in a foster home. With him gone, the bullying faded. But the damage had already been done. I carried the emotional scars long after the laughter stopped. That experience taught me a harsh lesson about trust, vulnerability, and how cruel people can be when they sense your innocence.

Years passed. We'd occasionally run into each other, once or twice a year. Then, when I was 17 and he was 19, freshly out of juvenile detention, we reconnected. I don't remember exactly how it happened—it just did. My mom, maybe believing everyone deserves a second chance, let him move in with us for about a month. At the time, I was working, trying to support myself and help my family. Theo didn't have a job or any plan. He spent his days lounging around the house and hanging out with my younger siblings. It wasn't all bad—we had some real moments of fun—but it didn't take long for cracks to show. One afternoon, while he was in the bathroom, his phone buzzed next to me. I picked it up and saw messages—lots of them—from other girls. My heart sank. I was working so hard, giving so much, and he was giving nothing back.

Even when we weren't living together, he wouldn't let me go. He'd call me late at night. Theo had type 1 diabetes, and when he was feeling down—or wanted to manipulate me—he'd stop taking his insulin. Sometimes he mixed drugs with it. His voice on the phone would be slurred, desperate, suicidal. At first, I'd panic. I'd call 911. But eventually, I realized this was a cycle—a trap. I couldn't keep saving someone who didn't want to be saved. Instead of calling 911, I started calling his grandmother.

Because, finally, I understood:

I couldn't keep sacrificing myself just to keep someone else alive.

2015: The Price of Secrets

At that time in my life, I was acting out a lot. I didn't really think about how my actions affected others. There was a girl in my grade named Luna, and we didn't get along. I knew her boyfriend had a reputation for being unfaithful, and out of spite, I started messaging him. We agreed to meet during a school event, thinking it would be easy to slip away unnoticed. He picked me up, and we drove to a secluded area surrounded by trees. What happened between us wasn't really about feelings—it was more about revenge. Afterward, while we were getting dressed, he tried to hand me a $20 bill. I froze. He quickly laughed and said it was a joke, taking it back, but I felt deeply insulted. I wasn't doing this for money. Still, I had done what I set out to do, so I let it go. We went back to the school and went our separate ways. I don't think I spoke to him again after that unless I had to.

A week later, I got called to the principal's office, where a Grey Birch County sheriff was waiting. I knew there was an age gap issue, but I stayed quiet. They questioned me about where I had gone during the event. I denied everything—until they showed me video footage of me leaving the school and getting into his car. I felt cornered, but I kept my responses vague. The officer told me plainly, "We know what happened. You're not old enough to consent." That's when the fear hit—not about the legal consequences for him, but about what would happen to me once Calvin found out. I didn't say anything more, but it didn't matter. After his girlfriend found out, the boy admitted everything, and his parents pushed for legal action. Even though I never made a statement or pressed charges, he ended up in juvenile detention. I don't know for how long, but that wasn't my focus. I had my own storm to face.

Walking home, I was filled with dread. I didn't know if the school had called already or if I still had time to come up with something. When I walked in, Calvin was sitting in the recliner watching TV. As soon as I saw him, I broke down crying. Calvin wasn't always cruel—there were rare moments when he seemed normal. He hugged me while I sobbed, confused. Through gasps and tears, I said, "A cop came to school today and said I had sex with someone, but I don't know what they're talking about." He told me he'd take care of it, whatever that meant.

Later, my mom got home from work, furious. She screamed for me to come downstairs, and I knew I was in for it. She and Calvin were both livid. "Why would you lie to me?" Calvin yelled. "I was about to go down there and raise hell thinking the cop was harassing you!" They hadn't known I was sexually active—they thought I was still a virgin. They began firing questions at me: "Did it hurt?" "Was it fun?" "Why would you do that?" "Did you use protection?" I lied through all of it. If they were this angry over one incident, how would they react if they knew this wasn't the first time? When they were done, Calvin shouted, "You're grounded for the entire summer!" As I turned to go back to my room, my mom added, "You're suspended from school for three days next week." So the school had called her after all. At that point in my life, getting grounded for long stretches wasn't new—but it never got any easier.

Snapchats & Statutory Lines

Once I started getting out more and meeting people, I began forming a loose group of friends. One of them was Harper, a girl from Bridgley. She wasn't the worst influence, but she definitely didn't encourage the best choices either. One afternoon, she texted me asking to hang out. I didn't have plans—rarely did—so I was in. I was about to ask my mom for a ride when Harper messaged again: "I'll come pick you up. Be outside in 10." I packed my backpack, slung it over my shoulder, and sat on the front steps. Ten minutes later, a blue Saturn clunker pulled up near the mailbox. Harper was in the passenger seat, grinning. Some guy was driving. I didn't ask questions—back then, I didn't feel like I had the right to.

Gas was cheap, and we did what most teens did: drove around the countryside with the windows down and the music too loud. The guy's name was Troy. He didn't talk much, just asked for my Instagram before dropping me off. Later that night, Harper blew up my phone. She was younger than me but acted older, especially when it came to boys. She told me that after they dropped me off, she and Troy had sex in his car.

She was practically giddy. She said he was 25, recently discharged from the military.

Over the next few months, Troy started liking every post I made. He added me on Snapchat and started messaging. At first, it was light—"How's your day?" or "What are you up to?"—until one day he asked if I wanted to hang out, just the two of us. He was gorgeous. Ripped. A gym body. Sharp jawline. Normal "fuckboy" haircut. And older—ten years older—but unlike boys my age, he wasn't afraid to be seen with me in public. That felt powerful.

We drove around, same as before, just talking. Then he started taking me places—community centers, little day trips. He made me feel wanted. He'd flirt and touch my legs under the bubbles in the hot tub, never flinching when someone recognized me. I liked the attention. I told myself it felt mature.

Eventually, we started having sex. At first it was in the car, tucked away on gravel roads. Then one day he brought me to his apartment—an upstairs unit above a café I hadn't even noticed before. From the outside it looked run-down, but inside it was all remodeled. He had a big sliding door I thought was so cool. His roommate was gone for the weekend, he said. So he stocked up on snacks and DVDs. We "watched" comedies, though mostly we just stayed in bed.

At the time, I didn't think much about what was wrong with any of this.

But over time, I started learning more. He had eight kids—yes, eight. From ages seven down to newborn. Then one day, casually, he said, "I want you to have my next baby. I get good military benefits." I laughed it off, but something in me paused. He told me he had a couple of statutory rape charges—said it was just from dating a girl whose dad didn't approve. I ignored the red flags. I was young. I was just trying to escape my home life. And I was getting attention. That's all that mattered to me back then. I stayed the weekend at his place, having sex until my body was sore. I wasn't in pain—I was just exhausted. He was smooth and strong, and part of me wanted to believe this was love. I didn't think about the power imbalance, or the way he used sweetness to blur the lines.

Anytime I called, he'd come. Even after I started dating someone else, he'd still message me. One day he DMed me on Instagram: "I'll be here when you guys break up. You always come back."

That was it for me.

I blocked him.

And this time, I never heard from him again.

2016: Steelboots and Sisterhood

I didn't have many friends in school. I was the weird kid—even before the drugs. Always a little offbeat, always just outside the circle. Eventually I found my way in, not through charm or sports or anything normal, but through my brain. I was smart, really smart, and I learned early that I could trade homework answers for things—Adderall, booze hidden in water bottles, whatever could get me through. That was how I started gaining traction with people. Not real friendship, not yet, but a kind of currency.

That's when Reed came around. At first it was just another transaction—I'd help with his assignments and he'd keep coming back. Slowly something shifted. He started hanging out with me even when there wasn't a paper due. We became inseparable for the next three years. He'd walk me home from school every day without fail. Once he got his license, he went out of his way to pick me up too— even when it meant driving across town. It was cheap back then, maybe $1.89 a gallon, and we'd fill up the tank and disappear for hours. Driving through backroads, windows down, music loud, being dumb teenagers, laughing about nothing. He had even upgraded to a Firebird which went a lot faster and did donuts a lot better. It was the kind of freedom I hadn't known I needed.

Over time our lives blended. We were at each other's family events, holidays, cookouts, always side by side. People would joke about us being more than friends, but it wasn't like that. Not for me. I was busy coping with my trauma in my own reckless ways, using sex with other guys like a bandage over a bullet hole. Reed? He wasn't part of that. He was my escape, my safe place—the only one I had back then.

There was one day that really stuck with me. We were walking home, just talking, and a car full of boys pulled up and started hurling slurs and shit at me. Before I could even react Reed was already moving. He yanked one of them out of the car by the collar and slammed him against the door, telling him to leave me alone. No one had ever done that for me before —not friends, not family. Just him. But like most things, it didn't last.

Once I got my own car, we started drifting apart. Still friends, but not constant. Then he met her—his first girlfriend. I could see he was tired of waiting around for me, wanting to settle down. She was a new girl from the next town over, pretty and mean with a sixth sense for who threatened her. She hated me instantly. She could see it, the thing Reed didn't want to admit: he was still in love with me since the day he laid eyes on me. She knew she couldn't compete. We stopped hanging out, which was fine at first. I had enough chaos to keep me busy. Then she turned into a problem—a real one.

My little sister had just started high school, seventh grade in our system, and this girl made her a target. One day she shoved my sister into a wall by the choir hallway—those jagged decorative bricks cut her arm open. The same night, she blasted my mom on SnapChat, calling her a whore. That was it. That was war. I woke up ready. Steel toe boots, tank top, hair pulled back—no way she was getting a grip on it—and tight pants with nothing loose to grab. I told my mom to keep her phone close because when I saw that girl, it was on. I got to school early, stalking the halls looking for her. She was dodging me like prey sensing a predator. But I had a second hour with her. She couldn't run forever. Right before class, I caught her by the choir room, inches from her face. "You got a fucking problem?" I said, loud enough to draw attention. She smirked and rolled her eyes. " I don't know what you're talking about." I stepped in closer. "You like putting your hands on little kids? I will put my hands on you."

Then—and this part still cracks me up—she tried to knee me in the groin. Like I was a guy? All she hit was bone, it didn't even faze me. I swung, fist, face, clean hit. I got a few more in before someone pulled us apart. She ran crying to the office. I stood there, steady. I had nothing to hide. The principal called me in. She told me she was proud of me standing up for my sister, but she had to suspend me or it would be her job on the line. She gave me In School Suspension (ISS) for the day and told me to stay home the next two. She made it clear my mom did not need to come in—probably terrified of the wrath she'd bring. Before I left, I made my rounds to collect homework. I walked into my sixth hour Family and Consumer Services (FACS) class, but it wasn't my class there—it was hers. I didn't care. I stepped in and asked for my assignment. "I got into a fight and got suspended," I said. The teacher blinked and asked why. I didn't miss a beat. "There was a senior beating up my seventh-grade sister." The room went quiet. Eyes on me, the teacher's expression shifted. "Well good for you," she said. "That's unacceptable. Here's your homework." I took the papers, turned on my heel, and walked out like a mic drop.

Standing Rock Standing Still

I met Dakota through my ex-boyfriend—who for whatever reason absolutely despised him. I'm pretty sure it had something to do with his skank of a baby mama. He made it clear I wasn't even allowed to speak to Kota. So naturally, once my ex and I broke up, Dakota was the first person I reached out to—mostly out of spite. No one was going to tell me what to do, especially not him.

At the time, I was 16 and Kota was 22. We started hanging out pretty much immediately, mostly floating between shady places and drug houses like the infamous "420 house" that was rented by two Native American stoners. That place was like a revolving door, with people coming and going all hours of the day and night. One of the guys who lived there would roll his own cigarettes and fill a cup with them and sell each for a quarter. It worked out for me since I was underage and couldn't buy my own anyway.

Dakota and I were together for maybe three or four months. It wasn't some epic romance— it was chaotic, impulsive, and mostly centered around hooking up in weird places. That was kind of the thrill of it. One morning, before I left for work my mom blew up on me. She was already suspicious of Kota, and I had told her he was 18 just to make the age difference less of a problem. Somehow she found out his real age. We argued, and in the heat of it, she said she was going to report him for statutory rape. I've never been a snitch, especially not over something that was her being petty and controlling.

I worked as a hostess at a little country cafe in town. I finished my shift that day, but I had no intention of going back home until I figured out what to do. Kota didn't have a phone, so I did the usual rounds, checking all the drug houses he usually hung around, but he was nowhere to be found. Desperate, I called up our friend Russ, who was closer to my age and always down to help. I picked him up and explained everything. Together we drove around looking for Dakota until we finally found him passed out on someone's couch.

The three of us came up with a plan. Kota had family in South Dakota who were protesting the pipeline that broke and spilled into the reservation's land and water. Police were not allowed on that area of the reservation, so even if she reported me as a runaway, the cops couldn't come get me. I was tired of living under someone else's rules, tired of the tension, and I definitely wasn't going to be responsible for sending someone to jail. It felt like the only option at the time.

Kota's idea was to head out to Cedar Bluffs—a rough, run-down town on a Native American Reservation known mostly for its public housing and heavy drug scene. The place always gave me anxiety. I was a 16-year-old white girl walking into a completely different world, and it never felt safe.

Before leaving the state, Kota said we needed to stop by a house so I could change clothes. I went into a backroom where this girl—who couldn't be over 14—handed me some clothes. Then she looked me dead in the eye and asked, "Wanna do an 8 ball? My mom tried hiding it, but I found it." I froze. I had smoked weed and snort muscle relaxers before, but that was it. I wasn't about to start doing hard drugs with some random kid in a stranger's house. Without saying a word I turned and stormed through the house, headed straight to my car. I yelled back, "If you're not in that car in the next ten seconds, I'm leaving you here!"

Kota jumped in without hesitation. I fired up my beat up five speed Ford Focus, tires spitting gravel as we peeled out. Russ barley made it—he drove in just as we were taking off. We drove Russ home in silence. It was a long, quiet 30 minute drive and none of us really knew what to say after the madness that just unfolded. Once we dropped him off, I pulled into the Walmart parking lot and emptied the last $150 from my ATM card.

That was all I had left to my name. Dakota said we were heading to Bismarck next. His girl best friend lived there and apparently he needed to see her. I didn't have any real plan of my own, so I was just along for the ride. I mean the drive. He didn't even have a license, and even if he did, I almost never let anyone else drive my car. Not that he would have known how to drive a stick shift anyway.

It was mid-November, and in the Midwest that's the start of the bitter cold. We didn't have money for a motel, so we parked in some hotel lot and tried to sleep with the car running on and off to keep from freezing. I wrapped myself in my hoodie and whatever clothes I had in my backseat, trying not to shiver myself awake every ten minutes.

The next morning, we made our way to Val's apartment. She greeted us like we were family, offered us a warm place to sit, food to eat, and introduced us to her boyfriend and toddler. It was a short visit, but it was one of the few moments on the trip that felt normal. Peaceful even. But we couldn't stay—we had a long drive ahead to Standing Rock.

Now I had never been one to get into serious trouble. I wasn't a "bad kid", just a little lost. But Dakota of course had different standards. We were low on gas and this was back when most stations still let you pump before you paid. He filled the tank with only $10 worth—but when he hopped back in the car, he told me "Go. Don't Pay." I hesitated, staring at him like he was kidding, but he wasn't. He just repeated, "Drive!" So I did. The gas station attendant came running out and even tried to stand in front of my car to stop us. I was terrified I was going to hit him. But Kota kept yelling at me to go, so I gunned it and sped off. I was shaking for hours afterward, sure we were going to get pulled over at any minute. It was a stupid, reckless thing for $10, but he didn't care and I wasn't in control anymore. I was just... following.

We made a stop in Fort Yates to visit his grandma. The neighborhood was something else—more like a camp of broken down shacks than houses. Everything looked like it was about to fall apart. Rez dogs ran wild, trash was scattered in every direction, and you couldn't take two steps without seeing a used needle or broken bottle. I stayed glued to Kota's side the entire time. His grandma, though, was kind. She welcomed us in and gave us supplies to make bologna sandwiches— something that, as gross as it sounds, felt like a feast. It was enough food to keep us going for a few more days. Before we left, we wanted to shower. Kota got in first and I was right behind him. I stepped in and immediately jumped back like I had touched a live wire. The ceiling was crawling with at least 30 cockroaches. I froze, and then scrambled back out, shivering as much from disgust as from the cold. That was the kind of shower that made you feel dirtier afterward than before.

An hour later, we were back on the road. The GPS said we were almost there. We started climbing a mountain, and when we hit the descent into the valley, it was like driving into another world.

I had never seen anything like it.

There were easily over 20,000 people spread out below—tents, tepees, flags from nearly every tribe in North America lining the road like a path into a different universe. There were massive communal tents for medical needs, dancing, food, and winter gear. Preparing for the snow that was already beginning to fall. This was the heart of the Standing Rock resistance, and whether I knew it or not, I had just driven into a major historical moment. Dakota's family had already set up a tent for us. We met up with them, gathered some donated blankets and gear, and spent the rest of the day exploring. Everyone we met was kind, curious, and generous. That night, we ate goat meat and rice. It sounded gross, but after barely eating for days, it tasted like heaven.

The longer we stayed, the more I started to change—physically and mentally. I was constantly dirty, covered in the same clothes, barely washing, and yet somehow I started to blend in. My pale skin darkened from dust and sun. We were still sneaking around for sex in our tent, even though it was freezing and there were no showers. I have no idea how we even wanted each other like that, but I guess when you're young and full of hormones, comfort and hygiene take a backseat to impulse and connection.

The only heat source in our tent was a small sunflower heater running off a green one-pound propane tank. One night the propane ran out while we were sleeping. I woke up with numb fingers and blue lips. It was -30 degrees outside. I shook Kota, told him we needed to change the tank, but he just grumbled and rolled over. So I tried to do it myself. When I reached for the heater, the plastic of the tent had melted from the heat and fused around it. My hand brushed against the scorching surface and I burned the entire top layer of skin on my hand. I bit my lip to keep from screaming. All I could do was pour water on it from a bottle and throw my gloves back on and try to go back to sleep with my hand throbbing under the covers.

The next morning, his aunt asked if I drove all of us, there was a house we could stay at for a day or two, about 45 minutes away. It had running water and a shower which, at that point, felt like luxury. As dirty as I was, and as much as I felt it, I didn't hesitate or complain, I just got behind the wheel. We pulled up to this tiny neighborhood in the middle of nowhere— maybe 10-15 houses total. The place was clearly rundown, like time had mostly forgotten it, but even then it was still a step up from Cedar Bluffs. Over the next two days I ate and showered more than I probably had in weeks. I must've showered ten times, maybe more—like I was trying to scrub off not just the dirt but also the past few months of my life. Same with food. I ate like I had never seen a full plate before. It was like my body finally got the message that it was safe—for now.

I still had my phone on me, even though I wasn't answering anyone. It was a straight talk phone which at the time was hard to trace, so I didn't feel too exposed. The only person I stayed in touch with was Clay. I trusted him with my life, since he had saved it so many times. I didn't tell him where I was—just that I was okay or at least trying to be. He didn't press me for more, didn't make me feel guilty or scared. He just talked to me like normal, like I was still me.

On the other hand, my biological father was leaving angry voicemails. He was never really around when I was growing up, always strung out on something—just like my stepdad had been. His messages were full of rage and threats, claiming he had FBI friends who were going to track me down. Said all kinds of cruel and harsh things, but that wasn't new for him. That kind of anger had been a background noise for most of my life. Honestly, I had no clue how any of this was going to end. I didn't even know what the next day would bring. It was survival, moment by moment.

Before we left for his aunt's house, we spent some time in this old school bus that had been converted into a weird makeshift apartment. It was pretty cool in a bizarre, post-apocalyptic way. There was a king-sized bed shoved into the back, with a couple tables, some old couch, and even a working fridge. It was like a hidden little world. We spent most of the time smoking with this white dude named Isaiah. He had gnarly, crusted up dreads and a sleepy vibe like he hadn't fully woken up in years. I thought we were just smoking weed, but looking back, I'm not sure that's all it was. I'd get so high that everything would go sideways—I'd start to feel loose, loopy, and then I'd black out.

At one point I was running out of cash, but I had a really nice set of subwoofers that were my mom's, and Dakota told me I needed to pawn them. Even though I thought I would never see her again, I still felt guilty for even thinking about it. After they all kept bothering me about it, I caved. We went to a pawn shop, but since we were in the middle of nowhere, he wasn't interested. Shoot, what are we gonna do? As we walked out, there was an old black guy standing outside the bar next door. He hollered over, "I will give you all the cash in my wallet for those subs." Dakota agreed for me, and he got $157.

His aunt had taken my car the entire time we were staying at the house. Just up and gone, said she was only going to the gas station, but she was gone for days—left us stranded. My mom had already reported my car stolen, so calling the cops would just tell them where I was. When she finally came back, she acted like nothing had happened, tossing us some clean clothes, blankets, and a few supplies. No explanation, no apology. We packed up quickly and got on the road, heading back towards camp. I was behind the wheel again, and despite everything, it felt good to be moving. We started descending the slope into the valley, approaching a line of cars stopped ahead on the highway. They were waiting to turn, and as I pressed the brake—nothing. No brakes. No resistance. Just the dead weight of the pedal going all the way down. Instant panic.

My heart jumped into my throat, but I didn't freeze. Thank God I knew how to drive defensively. I swerved around the stopped cars, missing incoming traffic by inches. Everything was a blur of metal and motion, but somehow we made it through. I immediately started downshifting, letting the engine slow us down from 65 miles per hour, gradually bringing the car to a crawl.

We pulled into the casino parking lot, more out of necessity than choice. My hands were shaking as I climbed out. I was the only one who knew anything about cars, so I dropped to the pavement and slid underneath to see what the hell just happened. And there it was—my brake lines had been cut. Clean through. I was stunned and furious. His aunt must've gotten herself into something shady during her "gas station run." Someone sent her a message, and I was just collateral damage. I wanted to scream, but I kept it inside. At least I had my car. We would deal with the rest later.

Eventually, we made it back to the protest land. This time we parked closer to the entrance, which was a first for me. Normally, I stayed on the outskirts, but we had plans to leave again soon- without his aunt this time. We walked around the grounds and for a moment, everything felt light. We watched the pow wow dancers move in rhythm, ate some food, laughed, and made jokes. It was the first time in a long time I had felt any kind of peace. Blissful even. But that moment didn't last.

As we headed back toward my car, I noticed a big blue truck parked nearly bumper to bumper with it. I made a joke —something like, "Damn, this truck is kissing my car's ass." We all laughed, but the laughter died instantly when I saw who was in the truck. My mom. She jumped out of the front seat, eyes wild and furious. She screamed, "Get in the truck NOW!" My stomach dropped. I didn't argue. I didn't even look around for help. I didn't even lift my head. I just walked to the truck, climbed in, and buckled up. Dakota was nowhere to be seen. No protest, no goodbye—nothing. He didn't try to stop it, didn't fight for me, just let me go.

Later, my uncle tried driving my car and realized it still had no brakes. I felt awful. It was a six-hour drive back to where we lived. What blew my mind was they found me in ten minutes when the police couldn't find me in ten days. It was just dumb luck.

That first hour of that ride was my mom screaming at me. I didn't fight back. Maybe I deserved it. Maybe I didn't. Either way, I just sat and took it. Eventually, I passed out—completely drained, the kind of exhaustion that goes bone deep. A few hours later, I woke up in some strange state. High, maybe, or cracked open emotionally. And we talked like nothing had happened, like it was another day. I didn't know how to feel.

At some point she was too tired to keep driving, and without saying much, she let me take the wheel for the last hour. I was surprised she trusted me to drive after everything. I guess she was more tired than mad—or maybe, in her own way that was her version of forgiveness. When I got home, everything became a blur. I don't remember much from those first few days—just fragments, flashes of moments stitched together by confusion and pain. What I didn't realize at the time was I was going through detox. My mom, overwhelmed and furious, essentially banished me to my room. Not that I was in any condition to leave it anyway. I was a ghost of myself—shaking, sweating, drifting in and out of sleep. My sister stepped in where my mom couldn't. She became my caretaker in those early days. Making sure I ate something, helping me get up to use the bathroom and how to function in general. She was gentle but firm, and without her, I honestly don't know what would've happened.

My mom was working two jobs and had little time—or patience—to nurse me through my crash. Her anger still hung heavy in the air, and I could feel it through the haze. I knew I had let her down, even if I didn't understand the weight of it. The detox lasted a little over two weeks. It felt like a lifetime—then one day, I managed to pull myself out of bed and walk downstairs. Almost like I had just woken up from a long, dark, unsettling dream. But it wasn't a dream. This was real. This was my life now, what I had to face, what I had to rebuild.

2017: Drunk, Dumb, and Drifting

Back then, I had a phone on and off—depending on whether I was working or grounded. When I didn't have service, I'd walk across town to the city center just to use the free Wi-Fi. I'd sit near the front doors, feeling the spring air while catching up on Snapchats and Facebook messages I hadn't seen in days. One afternoon, a small silver car slowed as it passed, then whipped around and pulled up beside the sidewalk. Inside were three guys from my grade, music blasting. One of them, Miles, leaned out the window and shouted, "Wanna come hang out?"

It caught me off guard—they usually bullied me at school, every chance they got. But now, here they were, grinning like we were old friends. One of them pulled out a bottle of Karkov vodka, and without thinking, I got in. Miles and his buddies Shane and Brad were already pretty lit, passing the bottle and laughing too loud. We drove aimlessly through the countryside for hours, the car reeking of alcohol and smoke. I didn't talk much. It felt strange—like I was someone else entirely when school wasn't part of the equation. Eventually we stopped at Shane's mom's house. They all piled out except one guy, and we sat in silence. Fifteen minutes later, they jumped back in and we took off again. A little while later, Miles said we needed to split up and grab his car. I followed his lead, still tipsy, still floating.

Miles and I switched cars. I didn't know where we were going, and honestly, I didn't care. Somehow, we ended up in the backseat. His lips were on mine. It happened fast—too fast. Time lost all meaning. I remember sitting up on the seat, him on his knees on the floor leaning into me, and then—suddenly—I reached up to wipe my nose.

That's when I noticed it. Blood. Pouring.

I froze. "Oh my God," I muttered.

Mortified, I looked down at the mess—vodka-induced or maybe just my body rebelling. Miles didn't flinch. He smiled, shrugged off his expensive gray winter jacket, and pressed it gently against my face to stop the bleeding. I couldn't even process what had just happened. I felt humiliated. We moved back to the front seat, and he drove me home. I remember staring down at my sweater, stained dark red, like something out of a crime scene. I had no idea how I was going to explain it.

When the Mouth Meets the Moment

As a teenager I was always pretty mouthy, always starting to start stuff or having something to say. I had been dating this little native guy named Tanner, who had a baby mama who was petty and kind of ghetto trailer trash. I was a cashier at the local Walmart, and I was working until 10 p.m. that night. My entire shift I had her and all her friends blowing up my phone about how they were gonna jump me. Every time I would go to meet up with her to fight, she would wait so long until I had to leave at curfew or just not show up altogether. That night I was just over everything, and I told them to pull up and that I was off at 10 p.m. My cousin Jaxon was also working the same shift as me, and he wanted to come out with me in case it got carried away. I had never been in a physical fight before this.

Outside, we went by the cart corral, and there were probably seven of them. All of them shouting and talking shit at me, but they wouldn't step closer. I handed my glasses to my cousin. I couldn't afford new ones if they broke. I leaned forward, put my hands behind my back, and closed my eyes. "I'm waiting?" They went silent. I opened my eyes after a few minutes and put my glasses on. I started walking past them towards my mom's truck to head for home since they weren't mad enough to finish what they started.

My cousin also was one to have a big mouth, and for some reason decided to argue with one of the guys. "I get so much more pussy than you!" he taunted. This guy had his pregnant girlfriend with and that hit the wrong nerve. Before I knew it, he had Jaxon on the ground throwing punches over and over again. Although my cousin did deserve it for opening his mouth, I wasn't going to sit there and watch him get the shit beat out of him. I pushed through the crowd, grabbed that guy by the forearm, and tried to pull him backwards. I saw red after this.

That guy's sister was also there. She grabbed my arm, trying to keep me from helping my cousin, and I swung around, grabbed her by both arms, and we tumbled to the ground at a downward slant. I had my keys in my hand since I was trying to leave, so as I was punching her, I also stabbed her a couple times with my key unintentionally. The only way I got stopped was because that pregnant girl grabbed me by my hair and pulled me on my back. By the time I was back on my feet, they were all running back to their vehicle and taking off. I ran over and helped my cousin up, and we checked out each other's injuries. There were a few red marks, and I had scratches all over my chest. I found it funny: that girl couldn't do anything but scratch me in a fight? What a pussy.

Learning to Bleed Without Cutting

When I moved out of my mom's house at 17, the world opened up—and not in a good way. Within a week of my birthday, we threw a party in a row of townhomes. It felt like the whole block was in on it. The old lady next door brought trays of Jell-O shots, and the other neighbors rounded up beer and booze like it was a potluck.

I had been talking to this guy, Tobias, for about a month and invited him. He was nearly ten years older, with a history that made people pause—he'd lost his leg in a freak accident, hit by a car while walking through a blizzard with his pregnant girlfriend. She and the baby died within 24 hours. He survived, barely, only to lose his leg to gangrene. People were sneaking him meth in the hospital. I didn't fully understand it then, but that kind of pain—theirs and mine—had a way of attracting each other.

When he showed up at the party, I was caught off guard. There was a knock, but no one was there—until I looked down and saw Tobias, beaming up at me. He pulled himself in, dragging his body across the living room floor to a chair. I felt obligated to be nice, but his presence made me uneasy. I escaped into the crowd. That's when I noticed a guy sitting alone at the table, rolling joints, not saying much. No drink, no smile—just watching. His quiet pulled me in. His name was Silas.

When I introduced myself, he simply said, "Come with me," and started up the stairs to my room. I followed. He knelt by my nightstand, pulled pills from his pocket, and crushed them into lines. "What is it?" I asked. He brushed his long black hair back and grinned. "Does it matter?" he said, almost laughing. I hesitated. "Chill—it's just a muscle relaxer."

That was enough for me then. Down the lines went. We lay on my bed, staring at the ceiling, talking about nothing, like we'd known each other forever. No touching, no pressure. Just silence and breath. That kind of calm was rare for me. Most men didn't come to my bed just to sleep.

Silas started showing up more after that. We bounced around with different people, mostly in basements and half-lit rooms. He crashed at Bailey's house—a kid who practically lived in his mom's basement. One day, Silas laid out a new line of powder. When I asked what it was, he said, "Coke." That's all I needed to know. From that moment, I was in. Cocaine gave me a rush that felt like freedom, like I was flying out of my own body. It became my drug of choice—and so did Silas.

Eventually, things between us blurred—sex, favors, rides, errands. I became his middleman, the one who made things happen while he stayed in the shadows. I was doing his work and sleeping in his bed. I thought it was love, but really, it was control disguised as connection. Silas had a way of disappearing, just long enough to wreck me. He'd vanish for days, weeks. I'd spiral. Sometimes his ex would message me, nasty and bitter, like I had taken something from her. Maybe I had—maybe we were all just fighting over scraps of his attention.

One night, coming down hard, we fought. I sat on the floor of my room, knees tucked to my chest, *trembling*. Panic swallowed me. When I was high and overwhelmed, I scratched. My face, my neck, my arms—until the skin broke and bled. It was the only way I knew to release the pressure.

Eventually, I started to see through him. I stopped dropping everything when he got out of jail. I blocked his numbers. I ignored his messages. But he always found a way back—burner phones, fake social media accounts, mutual friends' posts. It was like he couldn't stand to lose control of me, even though he never really cared for me. I was never more than an object—someone to use, to manipulate, to own.

Even years later, just hearing his name sent me into a PTSD spiral. It took *seven years* to break free—for real. Seven years of changed numbers, new accounts, cold silence, and ghost memories. Now, when I hear his name, I don't shake. I don't run. I'm free.

Burned from the Inside Out

For a while, I worked at a Holiday gas station as a cashier. Like most gas stations, we sold cigarettes, and if you looked under 40, you had to show ID. One afternoon, a guy came in to buy a pack of Montego Red Shorts. He was definitely under 40. When I asked for his ID, he fumbled through his pockets, but he didn't even have his wallet—just a $20 bill. "Ask Carmen, she can tell you my age! She's my landlord!" he said. Carmen was one of my managers, and I knew her well since she was my friend Brayden's mom. She also managed an apartment building, so I knew he wasn't lying.

"Fine. If I lose my job, I know where to find you," I replied. He finished checking out, but as he walked out, he said, "Maybe I'll invite you over for dinner sometime." That was weird. When I turned back around, he had come back and asked for his receipt. He wrote his number on the back with a highlighter and walked out with a smile. I was confused. I'd never been hit on like that before, but I was curious. We started texting, and before long, we really hit it off. We ended up dating on and off for about six months. I stayed at his apartment often, especially since my cousin was one of his roommates. At that point, I'd never gone through his phone; I didn't really have a reason to.

In the first month we started dating, he would take me cruising around the lake since the weather was still nice. One day, we got to talking about drugs, and I had the bright idea to try and score some cocaine. The only person I'd ever gotten coke from was Silas, and I knew that wasn't a route I wanted to go down again. I remembered my aunt's girlfriend was involved in the scene, so I reached out.

"Hey fam, can you hook me up with some snow?"

Within the hour, we picked up the girlfriend, Nova, and drove out to some lakeside cabins known for heavy drug traffic. We parked behind the cabins, handed her the money, and sent her in. About fifteen minutes later, she came back out. My eight-year-old brother was with us, so she casually reached her arm over the center console and handed me the bag, trying to keep it out of his view. We dropped her off before I even looked at what I'd bought. Then we took my brother home—he didn't need to be around any of that. Once we were on the road back to town, I finally pulled the bag out of the console, and my heart dropped.

"Um... I don't think this is coke," I said.

"What do you mean? Let me see," Milo replied. His eyes widened, and he slowly handed it back. "Well, you just spent fifty bucks—you might as well do it."

Didn't have to tell me twice.

We pulled into an automatic car wash. Once the colorful soap started covering the windows, I poured half the bag into a line and snorted it all in one go. Oh my God—it burned. I had never done meth before, so it hit me hard. We kept driving around for a while, but after about twenty minutes, I started feeling sick. I rolled the window down and instantly started puking down the side of his freshly washed car.

We went back to my house, and I ended up vomiting for most of the day. I was completely exhausted and couldn't keep anything down. Milo had to leave for his over-the-road trucking job the next morning, and I was stuck watching my roommate's son overnight. I was so drained from being sick that I decided it was best to bring the kid to my mom's for the night—I just couldn't take care of anyone like that. I stayed up all night with my sister Alex. She was always there for me—my ride or die. Around 3 a.m., I left to hang out with someone until about 5, then got ready for school like I did every morning. When I got to my mom's house, she was waiting—with a ten-panel drug test.

I tried to argue with her, told her I wasn't doing drugs, but she didn't buy it. I ran to the bathroom and asked Alex to pee in a cup for me to cover my tracks. But it didn't work—my mom followed me in and stood there while I peed. The results came back positive for amphetamines, opioids, Percocet, and weed.

My life felt like it was over.

Once I started being able to be around again at Milo's, there was one guy who was always hanging around, couch-hopping—Landon. I spent a lot of time with him whenever Milo was gone. He always seemed to flirt with me, but I was forward with everyone, so I wasn't sure if he was just messing around or if he really meant it. Landon was fun and knew how to keep things lively. One time, Milo and I were laying in bed during the day, and Landon came in. Both him and I ended up on the bed with our arms wrapped around Milo. Landon kept pushing his limits, reaching for my chest—testing the waters to see how far he could go.

A month or two later, Landon and I became inseparable. One night, he called me at 1 a.m., which was odd because he never called that late. I picked up, and the conversation started casual, but then he got serious. "So, I went into Anna's, and when I came out, my girlfriend was giving your boyfriend a blowjob in his front seat," he said.

I was furious, and without thinking, I blurted out, "Let's fuck. Come pick me up." I knew he didn't have a car, but I also knew he'd find a way. He ended up stealing Milo's car and left both of them behind. I snuck out of my house, and Landon picked me up. He put the middle seat down so I could sit next to him while he wrapped his arm around me. I felt like a giggly 12-year-old, just excited to be with him.

We ended up on a dirt road, just messing around. Landon seemed hesitant, saying, "I can't. This feels wrong," but I pushed the seat back and told him to shut up. I made the move, and we went all the way. Afterward, we went to his mom's house in Bridgley, where she made us bologna sandwiches. It was awkward because she knew Landon had a girlfriend, and I was definitely not her. Still, we ate the sandwiches, and then he drove me home.

I really liked Landon, and I was thinking about breaking up with Milo to try dating him. But a few days later, Landon started officially dating someone else, and I was left confused. Milo and I ended up breaking up a couple of weeks after that, but I had to go to the doctor first. That's when I found out I had chlamydia. I was 17 and had not been with anyone else in a long time except Milo and Landon, so I found out that Milo had been sleeping with his ex while we were together, and I had no idea. A year later, I found out Milo also gave me herpes, which, as you know, is lifelong and incurable.

The bloodwork also showed hepatitis C antibodies, which really threw everyone into a panic. I had to call my mom to pick me up from school and take me to the hospital for more blood tests. Of course, she yelled at me the entire time. She was furious, especially since Landon was an IV drug user at the time, and hepatitis C is often transmitted through blood. Landon insisted he didn't have it and promised to get tested. Turns out I actually gave chlamydia to Landon, who gave it to his girlfriend.

My mom then made me call Milo to come over. "Are you pregnant?" she asked, and I couldn't help but laugh at how ridiculous that sounded. He came over, and my mom sat us down on the couch, handing us STD pamphlets from the hospital. I tried not to laugh, but the guilt on Milo's face was enough to keep me quiet.

A few months later, I was at Milo's apartment cleaning up when he asked if I wanted to watch a movie in his room on his Xbox. I wasn't interested in hanging out with him—he had a girlfriend now, but I still agreed to go anyway. While we were in there, she walked in, clearly upset. "What the hell?" she yelled. I thought it was weird that she had access to the apartment, but she came in, acting psycho. We didn't do anything, but she still stormed off. Later, she came back, chewing me out about staying away from her boyfriend. I didn't care. I was sassy and wasn't afraid to do what I wanted, regardless of who he was with.

Sisterhood in Shambles

2019: Cracks Beneath the Surface

As time went on and I started dating Landon, I came to realize his sister Paige was the one who pulled me off a girl during a fight the year before. Great. I hated that bitch, but I would keep the peace for my boyfriend. After we first got sober she didn't have much to do with us, which was fine by me. We started slowly doing family gatherings and getting the kids together. Paige and I started talking more and eventually became pretty close friends. We would get together often even without the kids, drink, go shopping. We would even go to baby doctor appointments together. We were thick as thieves. She was my best friend for a year or so, but she wasn't always sunshine and rainbows, that's for sure.

In October of 2019, she had been living in Foxview in an apartment and there was a pub crawl at a hotel bar nearby. Me and Landon did a couples' costume, Cheech and Chong, the whole getup, facial hair and wigs too. Since it was a restaurant and bar it was easier to sneak in than an 18-year-old me could. It didn't last long, but I did get at least three drinks, which did it for me. Then the bouncer asked me for my ID. I used the excuse that I had it in my car and I would go get it. We walked out to the hotel lobby trying to get a hold of Paige, who was sucked into the crowd on the dance floor. We were staying at her apartment and couldn't go back without her. Eventually we got her to the lobby, and she was trashed, but that was the point of the night. Instead of being the best friend she claimed she was, she threw her keys at Landon and told us to go to her apartment, and that she was going to a party outside town. I was shocked. I'm not sure if it was the fact I had been drinking, but I got pissed and started to cry. I can't believe she would do that to me. I was petty and posted on my Snapchat story: "Got kicked out of the bar, at least I got wasted before they ID'd me, too bad my friends abandoned me." We got a ride back to the apartment and Landon and I started fighting because of how the night ended. She was such a bitch, and Landon did nothing to stand up for me. I was apparently in the wrong. This wasn't the only time she treated me poorly. She would be so nice to my face, because she was scared of me. I mean, she did watch me beat the shit out of her sister-in-law. She would say terrible things and try to be tough, but never in person.

There was one time I shared a post on Facebook that said, "Y'all ever had an Ex that went and dated a knock off version of you?" She screen-shotted it and posted it to her Snapchat story, but added the caption: "Bitch YOU were the knock off version with your infested stanky ass, I've personally seen better then you multiple times, IYKYK." (This was referring to Landon's long-time girlfriend, Sam, who was on drugs still and lost custody of her baby the second he was born.) We got both of us sober, into our own place, new vehicles, and a sweet baby boy, but she was better than me? Okay, lol.

2020: The Final Petal Falls

She got engaged and I was the first person she told. She even asked me to be her maid of honor with a cute little proposal box. Of course I said yes! From there we began hanging out even more, bridal shops for dress shopping and tux fittings, venue tours, decorations, and, like, everything else. My in-laws are very uppity and prudish, so I didn't really care to be around them much, but I was supportive of her. As she got further into wedding planning, they had a big influence on her decisions. To them I was chopped liver, which hurt my feelings, but it was her wedding, so I just went along with it.

One day she said she wanted two maid of honors, but that I would walk first still. I was so upset. I had put so much work into stuff for her. She wanted a pink party bus for her bachelorette party, so I started to plan it and got her guest list. I figured if everyone would pitch in $40, the bus would be easy to rent for the night. She did not like the idea of asking her friends and family to pay for it because it was the maid of honor's job to pay for it. She didn't expect her other "maid of honor" to pay for anything because she didn't have a job. How was I supposed to pay $900 for that? I had a new baby and I worked a minimum wage job, so that would be almost two weeks of pay. After this she blew up on me and said she didn't want me to be her maid of honor anymore since I couldn't do the job. Rage and hurt filled my body. We had our spats now and again, but I mainly tried to avoid her to prevent the drama. She talked bad about me to everyone in their family, which made them go from making me feel so welcome to an openly hated outcast. And they had no problems pointing it out.

Our son Noah was almost one, and he was supposed to be a ring bearer for Paige's son, who was six months older than him. They were to sit in a wagon and hold flowers. Since I had already bought my bridesmaid dress, I was going to wear it. Except I cut it in half to a knee-length dress and wore a pink and purple straw floppy hat to accent it, just to be petty and make a point. At one point Noah's grandma made a comment about my outfit. "Aw, that is so nice. You match the wedding party. How thoughtful!" She was so sweet. Since Landon and Noah were in the wedding party, we had to be there early for set up and pictures. I kept Noah busy, and I walked over and asked many times if they wanted Noah in any pictures with bridesmaids or groomsmen or what the plan was. I was told that once Paige's son woke up, Noah would be in the pictures. And so we started walking around just to pass the time.

I brought him into the bathroom to change his diaper, which took maybe five minutes. When we came out, her kids were taking pictures with the wedding party. This pushed me over the edge. She could hate me and be a bitch, whatever, it didn't bother me. But she deliberately left her own blood nephew out of the wedding pictures because she didn't like me? That was the shittiest thing she had ever done. I told myself once Noah was older, we could look at the pictures, and when he asked why mommy had pictures of him at the wedding but no one else did, I could tell him how horrible his aunt was. She even left him out of the pictures when he rode down the aisle in the wagon.

All of the years I was with Landon, she never backed down. It became less frequent, but in my opinion she was still the biggest cunt I ever knew. It wasn't about holding a grudge, not really. It was about protecting my peace, protecting my kid from being caught in the crossfire of something he didn't ask to be a part of. I knew where I stood with her, and I finally stopped trying to change it. There's only so many times you can extend an olive branch before you realize the other person's just sharpening it into a weapon. So I backed off. I didn't want to keep putting myself in a position to be disrespected, or worse, to react in a way I'd regret. Avoiding Paige altogether wasn't just avoidance—it was survival. It was my way of keeping the air clear for everyone else, even if it meant I had to choke down my own pride in silence. If Landon wanted to have a relationship with her, that was his choice, and I never stood in the way of that. In fact, I encouraged it. He and the kids deserved whatever bond they could build, free from the bitterness that I carried. But I knew my boundaries, and after everything I'd been through in my life, I had every right to keep them up. Some bridges aren't worth rebuilding.

He Let Me Drown, Then Threw Me a Rope

2018: Choosing Chaos

How did I start dating Landon? Well, it might sound a little toxic, but we went through hell together—years in the trenches—just to finally reach the light and bloom into something real. Toward the end of my relationship with Milo, we fought constantly. A lot of it was about Landon. Milo was jealous—how could he not be? Landon was my other half, in ways my actual boyfriend never could be. Eventually, Milo told me I couldn't see or talk to Landon anymore. I agreed—but only long enough for him to leave for work the next morning.

Landon met me in the stairwell of our apartment building that morning. He looked exhausted. When he pulled up his sleeve, I counted at least 15 needle marks from the night before.

"I couldn't handle the thought of losing my best friend," he said, shame heavy in his voice.

I hugged him—tight. The kind of hug where you can feel every emotion between you, unspoken but understood. I asked him what it felt like to shoot up compared to snorting, like I had done before. "Do you want to try it?" he asked, holding out one of those little plastic eggs from a quarter machine. Inside was something that looked like nothing, but we both knew it wasn't. Then he said, "Since you and Milo are always fighting, I'm heading to Moorhead to crash at my friend Tank's place. You could come stay with me, if you want." I paused. I looked around at what I had here—what I'd be leaving behind. But without my best friend, it didn't mean anything. "Yeah, why not?" I said. "Let me go pack a bag." He looked surprised—but he followed me anyway. I felt a rush of adrenaline, not from the drugs or the chaos, but from the unknown I was walking straight into.

The First High

Once we hit the road, Landon figured maybe we shouldn't go straight to his friend's place. We were planning to use, and out of respect for them—especially since his ex, Sam, had just gotten out of rehab—it didn't feel right. She was "trying so hard," apparently. Yeah... okay. So instead, we drove to the next town over where my cousin was crashing at his dad's house. We figured if I kissed enough ass, my uncle might let us stay the night. Somehow, it worked.

It was still midday when we picked up more dope. Once we got back, we locked ourselves in the bathroom. Landon got everything ready, filling the needle while I tied a sweater string around my arm. I was nervous—there's a lot that can go wrong with IV use. But I trusted Landon completely. He always made me feel safe, even in the most dangerous moments. And so, I shot up. Do you remember that early 2000s Nickelodeon show *Jimmy Neutron*? When he's deep in thought and you speed through different areas of his brain until—bam—the solution hits him? That's exactly what it felt like. The drug coursed through my veins and shot straight to my brain, and my eyes lit up like fireworks. It was intense. Terrifying. Euphoric.

Afterward, we jumped in the shower to hide any signs of what we'd just done. We were still high, and tried to have shower sex, but mostly just ended up knocking the curtain rod down... like, four times. We couldn't stop laughing. It was ridiculous and chaotic, but it was ours. All through that night, we hung out with my cousin while he played *Fortnite* on his Xbox. I lay on the floor, eyes tracing the beams on the basement ceiling, counting them one by one until morning came—and then we made our way to Eastmoor.

Once we got up to his friend's place, it was... nice. A little tense, but honestly, better than I expected. Everyone was welcoming and inclusive, which threw me off. Especially since I had ghosted Tank after a St. Patrick's Day date the year before. I thought it might be awkward—but no one seemed to care. Valentine's Day rolled around, and I woke up to this giant, bright pink stuffed dog, a box of chocolates, and flowers. I named him Jelly Bean. It was the first week, and I already felt like a princess. We decided to cool it on the hard drugs for a bit—not a full stop, just a pause. We were still smoking a ton of weed and chain-smoking Marlboro NXTs like they were air.

Beneath the Cotton

By April, I had surgery scheduled to get one of my wisdom teeth pulled. Landon came with me, and sat in the waiting room with my mom while I was under. Before they knocked me out, my mom stayed with me as they set up the IV and took my vitals.

"Why is your blood pressure so low?" she asked.

In my head, I thought, *Because I'm coming down, Mom.* But out loud, I said, "I'm just getting over a cold." Next thing I knew, I was waking up in a side room, completely disoriented. Some older nurse was holding me upright, trying to keep me from tipping over. I started crying. My mouth was full of cotton and gauze, my words barely audible: "I want my mom... where's my mom?" A few minutes later, she and Landon were there, helping me to the car. The surgeon handed my mom a paper prescription for hydrocodone—and mom refused to give it to me.

Shit, I thought. I had plans for those.

Later that day, I even called the dentist pretending I lost the script, hoping they'd write me a new one. No luck. They weren't buying it. *Damn.*

We ended up only staying with his friend for about a month. I even paid rent to help out, just to show appreciation. During that time, I started getting close with Sam—Landon's long-term ex. At first, I had my doubts. I remembered how they acted around each other back when I was still with Milo, and it made me uneasy. But Landon seemed completely infatuated with me, so I let it go. Somehow, we managed to convince Sam's grandma to co-sign for an apartment. It was technically hers—Sam's—because I was still 17 and couldn't be on the lease, and Landon was a felon, which disqualified him. So officially, it was her name on everything.

Dressed up for Disappointment

We were supposed to split rent and utilities evenly. I held up my end of the bargain—do you think Sam did hers? Nope. By the middle of our second month there, we were evicted. She didn't even try to get a job. I mean, she was 21 and I was 17. But who was the grown up?

Meanwhile, Landon was still doing outpatient treatment three days a week, court-ordered, and working at McDonald's the other two or three days. I picked up the slack wherever I could. His sobriety mattered to me—maybe more than my own at times. Sam's son, Axel, was living with us at the time. He wasn't even one yet, just a little guy—but so sweet. I loved that baby like he was my own. My Bubby.

Around then, we started going to Narcotics Anonymous meetings regularly. That's when I heard they were hosting an NA Prom. I'd only been to prom once before, and it was a disaster. Landon had dropped out in tenth grade, so he'd never been at all. It felt like a chance to rewrite something. One morning, I woke up and was playing with Axel on the floor. He crawled over to me, and I noticed his onesie. It read: *"Auntie Trinity, will you go to NA Prom with Uncle Landon?"* I hugged him so tight, tears welled up in my eyes. "Of course," I said—and when Landon came into the room, I kissed him with a long, deep kind of passion you don't forget. We found a prom dress on Facebook Marketplace and borrowed a suit—almost too small for Landon—from a woman we knew. He had never worn a suit in his life, and he did it just for me. Before the event, we even stopped at a park to take those classic prom photos, awkward poses and all.

The prom was hosted by a local LGBTQ NA group. I didn't mind—it felt like a safe space, a celebration of survival and self-expression. When we walked in, we quickly realized we were the only ones fully dressed up. Everyone else was in jeans or casual clothes. Still, person after person complimented us—our outfits, our vibe, the way we showed up for each other. For the first time in a while, I felt proud. Hopeful. Maybe I had a shot at prom queen. At my prom I was lucky to even have a date, let alone even be considered for prom queen. When it came time for the announcement, I was on the edge of my seat. But then someone else won. It wasn't like there was a prize, it was the point. My heart sank—but it turned to frustration when I saw who walked to the front: a man in a hand-sewn dress that looked thrown together, almost like rags. I felt furious. I'd poured so much into that night—our outfits, the effort, the emotion. And this? This felt like a slap in the face.

I wasn't used to the LGBTQ community yet—not in a hateful way, just unexposed. I believed people had the right to live their lives however they wanted. But in that moment, it felt personal. Like all that love and energy we had poured in was invisible. We stayed for the speech, clapped politely, and left right after. I didn't want to make a scene. But inside, I was burning. So much work. So much hope. And it felt like it was for nothing.

Shortly after prom, our time at the apartment was running out. We were handed a three-day eviction notice, and I had no idea where we were going to go—or what we were going to do. *Fuck sobriety,* I thought. *Why does it even matter anymore?*

Everything Hurts, So Nothing Does

After I had my second wisdom tooth surgery, we didn't want to use around Axel. I would never endanger a child like that, so we crashed at a crack house for the night. Just a small apartment, barely furnished, chaos behind every closed door. In a spare room, on an old futon, we did what we always did. Same high, same rush—except this time, Landon gave me a little more than usual. At first, we brushed it off. Started kissing, the heat building like it always did, planning to have sex. But within five minutes, something changed. I got incredibly nauseous. Dizzy. Everything tilted. I pushed him off me and tried to get to the bathroom—ten feet away—but my legs buckled in the hallway. Landon ran up behind me, catching me just in time and helping me inside. I collapsed by the tub and started puking. Violently. Uncontrollably.

It was a small place. Thin walls. Everyone could hear me.

Landon stepped out and awkwardly said, "It's the anesthesia from her surgery today... it's messing with her." We both knew that was a see through lie. Everyone else knew it too. I don't remember how long I was in that bathroom. It felt like days, but it was probably just a few hours. My body was wrung out. That wave of sickness—it was the exact same thing that had happened the first time I used meth. Maybe I'd gone over my limit. Maybe my body was rejecting it. I didn't know. I just knew I was high, sick, and completely drained. When it finally stopped, all I wanted to do was lay down. We'd promised we'd never get high without each other. That this was something we'd always do together. We were a team.

The next day, we shook it off. Grabbed something to eat, tried to act normal, and headed back to the apartment—only two days left before we were out. We stopped by the liquor store and picked up the biggest, cheapest bottle of vodka we could find. Fuck it, right? I posted something on Facebook, probably half a cry for help, half just venting. My cousin messaged me—well, not really my cousin, but her mom had been best friends with my mom for over twenty years, so it counted. She said we could crash at her place for a while, at least until we got back on our feet. That afternoon we packed up what little we had. It didn't take long—we'd already lost or left behind so much. We were just moving across town, but it felt like crossing into another life. Again.

That night, we decided to go out with a bang. Sobriety was a joke at that point. We were about to be homeless—why not go hard? We lined up plastic shot glasses and filled cups of water to chase them. Not a good chaser, but it was all we had. We put on "Turn Down for What" by DJ Snake and played a game—take a shot every time they said the word "shots." Stupid? Yeah. But it felt like something.

I was still coming down off the last high, so the vodka hit me fast and heavy. I got sick again. Ended up hunched over in the bathroom, puking my guts out. When I finally stopped, Landon came in and got in the shower with me, helping clean me up. The rest of the night is mostly a blur, but even through the haze, we still had sex for hours. It didn't make sense—but that's what we did. Even in chaos, we clung to each other like it was the only thing keeping us from disappearing completely. After that night, the hangover hit hard—physically, emotionally, all of it. We started leaning toward actually getting sober. I didn't know how much more my body could take. Everything felt worn down—my nerves, my stomach, even my skin. Something had to give. We moved in with my cousin. She was weird, but cool in her own way. Her boyfriend? Just weird. But they gave us a roof, and that was enough.

McMornings and Military Trucks

We were still working. Landon had finished his outpatient program, which meant he could pick up more shifts. He didn't have a license, so his car and insurance were both in my name. He usually worked the 5 a.m. shift at McDonald's. He liked the early morning crowd—the little old folks who came in like clockwork, and had their black coffee and breakfast sandwich. Said they made the mornings better. That morning, he kissed me goodbye and left for work. Minutes later, he walked back into the bedroom and shut the door behind him. Still half-asleep, I squinted up at him. "You're gonna be late for work," I mumbled.

"Um... you should look outside," he said, voice low. "I'm not going anywhere."

What? It's 5 a.m. I groaned and dragged myself to the window, rubbing my eyes as I pulled back the curtain—then froze.

Outside, it looked like a scene straight out of a war movie. SWAT officers in full gear were walking down the street, machine guns in hand. Military vehicles blocked off both ends of the road. Sirens in the distance.

Lights bouncing off windows. The whole damn neighborhood was on lockdown.

Holy shit.

Landon called into work and texted his boss a picture of what was unfolding outside our window. No way he was making it in that morning. They stayed out there most of the day. Turns out someone had shot their spouse in a garage a few houses down—some messy domestic nightmare. It was wild, like the world was just as chaotic outside as it had been inside us for so long. Then one day, the kind of miracle you only get once in a lifetime happened. Landon got a call from a weird number—he almost never answers those. But for some reason, this time, he did. Fate, maybe?

Hope, Delivered by Mail

It was his great-aunt Rita. Wicked woman. When his grandpa started slipping into dementia, she convinced him Landon was no good. Got him kicked out, made him change the will. That betrayal stuck with Landon for years. His grandparents had adopted him—they were his everything. His grandpa was his hero, his whole world. And she stole that from him. So hearing her voice? Yeah, that was a shock. She wasn't calling out of guilt or kindness, of course. The only reason she called was to let Landon know there was a life insurance policy about to expire—and only *he* could claim it. She'd been fighting for it for years, ever since his grandpa died. But the money was his, and she knew it. One call turned into a process, and a month later, a check showed up in the mail.

Twenty. Thousand. Dollars.

It felt like his grandpa was watching from somewhere else—like he saw us drowning and finally threw us a rope. We were saved. We could finally breathe. Finally *start* our life. We each got a new vehicle—well, new to us. Landon picked out a 1999 Dodge Ram ¾-ton diesel truck, and I got a 2008 Saturn Aura. We felt like royalty. From there, we did what we had to do—got ourselves into a place of our own. Then came the essentials: furniture, dishes, clothes, the whole setup. It was finally happening. We were finally building something real.

We'd been trying for a baby for almost a year—ever since that first pregnancy scare in the very first month. After that, Landon swore up and down that if I ever got pregnant, he'd take care of me and our baby. Funny thing is, he used to HATE kids. Take Sam's son, Axel. She used to swear up and down he was Landon's, and he wanted nothing to do with that. When Child Protective Services took Axel away the first time, they tried to give him to Landon, and that was the farthest from what he wanted. Then the DNA test came back like it was straight off *The Maury Povich Show*: *"You are NOT the father!"* He was relieved—wanted to move on. But with me? He was different. Gentle. Committed. I felt so in love, like maybe this was the real thing.

When fall came, my ovulation app reminded me the test date was coming up. I still had a couple tests left over from the previous months. I didn't think it would happen—I've had so many uterine issues, so many reasons to doubt—but I tried anyway. I took the test, left it in the bathroom, and walked away. Five minutes. I couldn't bear to sit there and stare at it, so I waited in the other room, pretending I wasn't checking the clock every ten seconds. When I finally went back, I thought I was imagining it. A line. A *faint* line, but it was there. My heart shot up in my throat. I ran into the room with the test in hand, breathless. "Look!" I said as I showed it to Landon. He didn't believe me. So I took another. Same thing. Another. Still faint lines—but they were all there.

Could it be a false positive? We didn't want to get our hopes up, so we went to Urgent Care for a blood test. We sat in the waiting room, nervous energy bouncing between us like static. I had the My Chart app, so I usually saw the results before the doctor even came to get us.

Ding. Results in.

I opened it, and my breath caught.

Positive. I was already around eight weeks.

2019: Under the River Sky, We Were Still Just Kids

We were stunned. Elated. Everything slowed down at that moment. We went home and did a little photoshoot to announce it—just us, the faint pink lines, and a whole new kind of future waiting quietly on the other side. The following weekend, my 14-year-old sister Alex came to stay with us. She spent more time at our place than she did at home—it was like we were her escape. After the news about the pregnancy, Landon wanted to celebrate, and his idea of celebrating usually involved drinking. Alex started bragging about how she could hold her liquor, trying to act grown. Landon, never one to back down from a challenge, called her bluff. He grabbed a liter of Fireball and, for some reason, thought water would be a good chaser. I don't know what he was thinking—like we hadn't just learned the hard way that this never ends well.

The music got loud, the laughter even louder, and before we knew it, we were on an adventure to the park across town by the river. I couldn't drink—I was pregnant—but they were running around like little kids, wild and free. At one point, we lost Alex. It was pitch dark, no lights, just the hum of the river in the distance. We finally found her squatting in the middle of an open field, peeing without a care in the world. That was my cue—it was time to take them home.

Whiteout Loyalty

As time passed, we found ourselves creeping into our first winter in our own apartment. I was about five months pregnant and starting to really show. Landon was working at an assembly warehouse at the time, and some of the people he worked with were... questionable, to say the least. One night around 10 p.m.—in the middle of a full-blown blizzard—he got a call from his friend Joel. Of course, Joel was stuck in a ditch on some random back road, coming back from a casino. Why was he out in this type of storm, you ask? Crackheads, that's why. Landon had already been drinking, and everything in me wanted to say no. But I was scared—scared that if I didn't go, something bad would happen to him. That's how things worked with us: chaos wrapped in loyalty. So Landon, Alex, and I piled into our big truck, ignoring every "no travel advised" warning just to save some crackhead friend in the middle of nowhere.

By the time we got close, the storm had gotten worse. Along the way, we ended up helping a farmer who had a trailer in the ditch. That random act of kindness ended up saving *us*. When we finally got to Joel's car and tried pulling it out, our back end slid right into the powdery snow and got stuck. Now we were the ones stranded. We sat there for what felt like forever, the windshield wipers scraping across frozen glass, leaving marks we could barely see through. Luckily, the same farmer we helped earlier lived up the road. He showed up like a guardian angel with a skid steer and pulled us out. I was beyond grateful—but also terrified. No way were we staying out there. That's how horror movies start.

I made Landon drive us home. What should have been an hour-long trip turned into five hours of navigating in total whiteout conditions. The road disappeared, and the only way he knew where to go was by following the GPS line inch by inch. At some point, I finally passed out. I couldn't hold my eyes open any longer. When we pulled into the driveway, it felt like waking up from a nightmare you somehow survived. I was scared, angry, and exhausted—but we were home, and that's all that mattered.

Just a Little, He Said

Things settled back into a rhythm after that—well, if you could even call it that. Landon and I always seemed to be fighting about something, and being pregnant with a flood of hormones definitely didn't help. He was jealous of my past, the exes that came before him. I had a pretty long history, and he couldn't let it go. His drinking didn't help either—mostly Fireball, which always lit a fire under his ass. I was working as a receptionist at a knockoff hair salon inside the sketchiest Walmart I'd ever seen—straight up in the middle of the ghetto. Toward the end of my pregnancy, I cut back to just three or four days a week because I was constantly exhausted.

One of my days off, I woke up with a weird off-feeling in my gut. Nothing specific—just that creeping sense that something wasn't right. Landon said he didn't want to go to work because he wasn't feeling good. Fine. But he mentioned he was still going to give Joel a ride and would be back in 30 minutes. I laid back down, figuring he'd be home soon. After a while, I heard him come in quietly and head straight for the bathroom. That off-feeling I had? It spiked. My whole body knew before my mind did. I waited a minute so he wouldn't hear me and walked in. There he was—caught like a deer in the headlights. A small bag of meth clutched in his hand.

I was so pregnant. So vulnerable. My heart dropped. *Are you serious right now?* I thought. He just stood there, eyes low, guilty as hell. "I was just gonna do a little and flush the rest," he said weakly. I held out my hand. He set the bag in my palm like it burned him. I didn't say anything—I couldn't. I walked out, shoved it inside a Midol bottle, and scrubbed my hands raw in the sink. I couldn't believe I let that touch my skin. After a while, I flushed it. Quietly. Without a word. It wasn't worth the fight. But what did I want my child's life to look like?

Forgotten Until it Wasn't

After that moment in the bathroom, things started to shift. Slowly—but they did. Landon began to get his act together, and for us, that was a huge milestone. One of his friends got him a job at a construction company. The hours were long and the work was tough, but it was a step up from anything he'd done before. Plus, he got to work side-by-side with his buddy every day, and that made it easier. He did so well, they gave him two raises that year—big ones. And over the next couple of years, they just kept coming. They respected him. He worked hard, moved up fast, and it finally felt like we were getting somewhere solid.

Of course, things couldn't stay on track for long. One day, while I was at work, Landon called me at 10 a.m.—which was unusual because he should've been working. I rushed to the back of the building to answer, thinking something was wrong. The sound of him crying immediately made my heart race. He kept saying, "I'm sorry" over and over again. I tried to calm him down, hoping I could understand what happened. "What did you do?" I asked, bracing for the worst.

"Her," he said. And I knew exactly who he meant.

I immediately told my boss I had to leave. I rushed to meet Landon in the parking lot and made him tell me everything.

It was during our first week of dating. When we had fought while we were both high, Landon had left. He'd picked her up, and they had sex in the car. The same seat I'd been sitting in for over a year. Two days later, he gave me all those Valentine's gifts. She took him shopping, and they both were okay lying to my face that day and all the days after that. I called her. She didn't try to deny it—she just said, "I'm sorry." Sorry? That wasn't enough. That would never be enough. Landon claimed he'd forgotten about it until that moment, that it just "came back" to him. How could you just forget something like that and go on loving someone with no guilt?

Who would believe that bullshit lie? Not me. I was crushed. I spent days crying, completely lost, trying to figure out what the hell I was supposed to do. Eventually, I gave Landon one last shot—strict boundaries, no more chances. If he slipped up again, I was out.

But her? She didn't get another chance. I was stunned. Sam looked me in the eye and told me she had been my best friend every single day

132

for over a year—with this eating away at her the entire time. The betrayal hit different. The thought of her made my blood boil.

From Labor to Learning Curve

A few months after he started the job, it was time—our baby was coming. Landon had just worked a 12-hour shift, and this little one was in no rush. I ended up in labor for 27 hours. I only pushed for an hour, but the whole thing was brutal. There were complications that scared the hell out of Landon. He didn't know what to do—hell, he never liked kids before this. The epidural dropped my blood pressure so low that I lost consciousness. Suddenly, it was chaos. They couldn't find our baby's heartbeat, because the sensors weren't picking anything up. I couldn't move the lower half of my body, and that made it all worse—I felt powerless. Nurses rushed in, flipping me side to side, trying everything they could. Nothing was working. By the end of it, I was pushing all natural. The pain was beyond anything I could've imagined—violent, raw. I screamed until my throat burned, tears streaming down my face, holding onto Landon's arm so tightly I nearly tore it off.

And then—at 9:01 a.m.—he was here.

Our beautiful baby boy. 7 pounds, 2 ounces. Big ol' cone head.

A couple days later, we were discharged and heading home. And I don't think I've ever been so happy to see our little apartment. It wasn't much, but it was ours. And now it was his, too. From there, we did what we could to survive. We had no idea how to be parents, but we figured it out day by day. When Landon got laid off during the winter, he stayed home with the baby. It was a learning curve for him, but he did his best, and that mattered. By the fall, we moved into a bigger apartment so our baby could have his own room. I started working on my credit—any way I could. Never missed a single payment. But we were still living in the worst part of Eastmoor, the kind of place that made your skin crawl. A woman had her baby cut out of her over there. A teenage girl was found chopped into pieces. Stories like that were endless. It wasn't just unsafe—it was hell. And it was no place to raise a child. We had to get out.

2021: Out of the Darkness, Into a Home

Our house search was actually kind of fun. Our realtor, Nancy, was a sweet older lady who specialized in rural properties. That was exactly what we wanted. After everything we'd seen, we didn't want to be anywhere near a city. We finally found a place right in our price range—$69,000. Three bedrooms, one bath, a double-stall garage that was heated. It felt like it was meant for us. There was one hiccup in closing: the city had to pass a levy. If they didn't, we'd have to pay an extra $3,000 up front—just to get it refunded a few weeks later. We couldn't afford that, so while we waited, we moved into a small apartment attached to my mom's shop. It was temporary, just until the paperwork came through.

Thank God we did. When I went back to our old apartment to grab the fancy shower head we'd installed, I saw something I wish I hadn't—a broken 40 oz. beer bottle, blood everywhere. No idea what happened there, but I was just grateful we weren't around when it did. The house ended up being in my name only. Landon still had things in collections, and the lender wouldn't allow both names on the mortgage. Honestly, it was a hidden blessing. I had good credit, and with the market the way it was, I locked in a 3% interest rate—practically unheard of. And just like that, we were moving into our first real home. A place of our own. A fresh start. A brand new chapter.

The Last Slip

By 2021, we were finally settled into our home. Landon's friend
Tank was staying with us for the season so they could ride to work
together—Landon had a company truck now. On a crisp fall day, Landon
spent the afternoon drinking with his buddies like usual. I had Noah with
me, and it was getting late, so I packed up and headed home. I was
working on my Associate's in Criminal Justice and had a paper due. Tank
said he'd bring Landon home later. No big deal. It was a two-hour drive,
and once I got Noah to bed, I sat down to write. But after three hours, I still
hadn't heard from Landon. That wasn't like him—he got clingy when he
drank. I tried calling. No answer. Something felt off.

I called Cora, the wife of one of his friends. "Hey, Landon isn't
answering. Everything okay over there?"

"Um... I'm in the bathroom. I'll call you back in a few minutes after I
check."

That didn't sit right, but I tried to focus on my paper.

When her name popped up on my phone again, my stomach dropped.

"You're gonna need to talk to Landon," she said, and passed him the phone.

He was sobbing. I couldn't make out much, but I heard the word *smoked*. Then I thought he said *H. Heroin*. My blood boiled. I threw Noah in his car seat, called my mom with a rushed explanation, and told her I'd be dropping him off. Then I grabbed the biggest crowbar I could find. This was war. When I pulled back into the driveway I had just left five hours earlier, I didn't hesitate. I had one question: *Where's Dean?* Colt's dad—the one who gave him the drugs.

"I'm not ready to talk to you yet," I snapped at Landon. "Where is he?"

I stormed into the house, but Dean was hiding behind a locked door.

"Respectfully, Colt, if you don't open this door, I will break it down. And I know you're renting—so let's not."

Colt managed to get the door open. I charged in, crowbar in hand, and pointed it straight at that old man's face. "Who the hell do you think you are? He was *sober*! You just blew up his whole life for what—fun? You're a grown man. You *know* better." He tried to lie—said he didn't give Landon anything. But the truth came out fast. Colt found a meth pipe and a baggie hidden under his dad's pillow.

Meanwhile, Landon—overwhelmed and ashamed—punched a full propane tank off its blocks. I don't know how he didn't shatter his hand. I walked back outside to find all our so-called *friends* sitting on the porch like spectators at a circus. "You!" I pointed the crowbar at each one of them. "You call yourself his friends? You let this happen?! *Tank*, you were supposed to watch him!"No one said a word. I loaded Landon into the car and started driving. We argued the whole way home—he even tried to jump out while I was going 65 mph. I couldn't do it anymore. I couldn't risk Noah's safety. I dropped Landon off with Tank and drove straight to my mom's. I curled up with my baby and held him like I never wanted to let go.

The next day, I was still steaming. I sent my uncle to check the house and assess Landon for damage. That's when I found out it wasn't heroin—it was meth. I mean, not much better, but given Landon's history, it felt like a small relief. I nearly packed up and moved to Texas right then and there. But I took a deep breath. I didn't run. I faced it. When I got back home, the storm wasn't over. We cried. We screamed. We said every hard thing that needed to be said. But in the end... we stayed. And he *meant* it when he said he wanted to change. He never touched hard drugs again. He made it.

2022: You Didn't Feel Him Leave

Time went on, and we continued to grow. Landon kept moving up in his career, proving his worth year after year. I finished my first degree. For a while, things felt like they were finally going right. We were steady. Happy. But nothing good ever seemed to last forever for us. One day, I was overwhelmed by emotion. It came out of nowhere—I couldn't stop crying, couldn't get a grip. I thought maybe I was just tired or getting sick. I was at my mom's and decided to take a shower, hoping to pull myself together.

I sat at the bottom of the tub, letting the hot water run over me. But something felt off. A dull cramping started in my abdomen—not sharp, but... wrong. And then, just like that, it happened. A blood clot, the size of a golfball, slipped out with the water and into the tub. Everything stopped. The world. Time. My breath.

That wasn't just a blood clot.

I knew in my soul...

I had just lost a baby.

The pain that ripped through me was like nothing I'd ever felt before. It was physical, emotional, spiritual—all-consuming. Somehow, I got dressed and made it to my car, where I called my aunt Zoe. She was deeply religious, and I needed someone to make sense of what just happened—someone who could talk to God for me, because right then, I couldn't. Between sobs and screams, I choked out, "How could He do this to me? Why would God take my baby away?" She tried. She told me it was part of God's plan, that everything happens for a reason. But no words could fill the hole in my chest.

I *knew* it was a boy. I named him Owen.

And I mourned him with everything I had.

When I got home and finally talked to Landon, I told him what happened. He looked at me, confused, and said something I'll never forget: "Why are you so upset over something that wasn't even really a baby yet?" That shattered me. How could he not feel this too? Maybe it was different for him—maybe because it hadn't grown inside of him, because it hadn't *left* from his body. But for me, Owen was real. That grief built a wall between us.

We didn't talk about it much after that. Things on the surface were fine, but deep down, I couldn't let it go. And he just didn't understand. After losing Owen, we stopped trying to have another baby. I was too torn up to even think about it again. That spring, during clean-up week, we got rid of all our baby stuff. I knew it wouldn't be happening anytime soon—and I needed to let it go, at least for now.

I even got a tattoo—one for Owen, and one for our dog Diesel, who we had to put down that fall. They are sitting on a cloud together. It felt like the only way I could carry them with me.

Save the Date, Change the Date, Screw the Date

When Landon and I first started dating, I told him straight up: I would *not* be someone's girlfriend forever. I'd seen my mom's friend waste eleven years with a man who eventually admitted he'd only stayed so she could raise his daughter. That wasn't going to be me. Time passed. Life moved on. And then it was our fourth anniversary—February 7, 2022. We had just finished having sex (because, hey, four years is a big deal), and I rolled over to grab my glasses. I can't see anything without them—literally nothing more than an inch from my face. Out of the corner of my eye, I noticed Landon kneeling by the bed. Butt naked. I squinted. Was I seeing this right?

I leaned closer. "Is this a joke?" I said. "Because if it is, it's a shitty one." But he was holding a ring. And then he said, "No, this is real. Will you be my wife?" I lunged forward and hugged him so hard we almost toppled to the floor. I had been waiting for this moment since the day I met him. Through all the chaos, heartbreak, laughter, and love... this was our moment.

And what a story it is.

Then came the whirlwind of wedding planning—dress shopping, decor, invites, and everything in between. For six months, my life was a blur of Pinterest boards, phone calls, and decisions I didn't even know I'd need to make. And then, right before my bridal shower, I found out I was pregnant. I was terrified. We had just gotten rid of all our baby stuff that spring, and after losing Owen, I couldn't handle going through that pain again. I was overly cautious—watching every symptom, avoiding every risk. The first trimester was miserable. I was so sick I had to work half days, just to manage enough energy to drag myself off the couch. It was rough.

We originally planned to get married in May 2023. It was going to be huge—the kind of wedding I'd dreamed about since I was a little girl. But nothing, and I mean *nothing*, went as planned. A few months after sending out save-the-dates, my grandma decided to sell her house. That house was our wedding venue. And then, to top it off, some of Landon's extended family (who I'd met maybe three times in five years) tried to tell me I couldn't have my wedding that day—because they'd be on vacation. I couldn't believe the audacity. Landon hadn't even talked to them before I came into the picture, and now they thought they could make demands?

No. Just no.

By some mix of impulse and divine timing, I already had my dress. And I happened to know the owners of the bar in the next town over. So, we said screw it—we moved the wedding up by *eight months*, to September 2022. No big production. No broadcasting it. Just our closest friends and family. Everyone else? They could suck it. And honestly, once I stopped letting other people push me around, things started going so much smoother. We cut our wedding party down to just a maid of honor and best man—and our flower grandmas, of course.

Left at the Altar—By My Best Friend

My maid of honor was Aria, a friend I'd met when we moved into our house. She lived just down the street, and we were practically inseparable. Our kids were close in age, and if I wasn't at her place, she was at mine. We laughed, we cried, we lived life together—until she blindsided me. Ten days before the wedding, she sent me a message on my way home from work:

"I don't think I can be your maid of honor. I mean, I don't even really know you—we've only been friends for like a year. And I told you I don't do speeches."

Are you *joking*? After everything? I had gotten *ordained* and married her and her husband—and she couldn't stand up with me at my wedding? But I didn't have time to sit and sulk. I had a wedding to pull off. Around that time, Sam had come back into the picture. I had let her back into my life despite the past. I mean, I was getting married, so why hold on to all that? She was sober, and after all the years I'd held space for her, I asked her to step in as my maid of honor. Let's just get this thing done.

The wedding itself went pretty well. My Aunt Zoe married us, which made it all the more special. There were heartfelt speeches from loved ones that brought tears to my eyes. In that moment, it didn't matter who didn't show up—it was about who *did*. The people who stood beside us, who'd been through it all. That was what counted. A week later, we set off for our honeymoon in Las Vegas. Thanks to some generous gifts and smart budgeting, we had about $1,300 left over to play with. Oh, and I can't forget the biker rally that came through unplanned who lit up the party. Not bad for a quick getaway.

We stayed at what can only be described as a roach motel in a very questionable neighborhood—but that's honestly what made it great. It had character. And 24/7 security, which helped calm my nerves, especially with my emotions running high and me being pregnant. We did a lot of walking—which wasn't ideal in my condition—but it was worth it. We visited the Heart Attack Grill and wandered down Fremont Street, taking in the wild energy of it all. But the *best* part of the trip was the Saw Escape Room. It was set up in a creepy old warehouse, modeled exactly after the movies, and I had made sure to binge-watch all of them before we left so everything was fresh in my mind.

Buried Beneath Survival

It was just me and Landon, and there were four rooms to get through. I was *on it*. Puzzle after puzzle, I took the lead—Landon was too squeamish and half-convinced it was real. Meanwhile, my pregnant butt was crawling through cages full of bloody pig heads, shoving my arm into a garbage disposal, and locking myself inside a cremation machine. I was kicking ass. We completed three out of the four rooms within the time limit, and the staff was genuinely shocked. Most groups of ten don't even get that far. They were blown away. For the rest of the trip, we played a game:counting how many prostitutes we saw. By the end of day four, we'd tallied up 27. Vegas is... something else. By then, I was more than ready to come home. I missed my own bed and some sense of normalcy. But it was a trip we'd never forget.

Once winter set in, my hormones went wild—my sex drive skyrocketed. Freaky became the new normal. Landon and I had talked before about wanting to try a threesome—something I had never done—but the big issue was finding someone who would respect our boundaries. Someone we could trust to stop if things got weird. Landon suggested Sam—his ex. I know how that sounds, but honestly, at this point in our friendship, she had proved herself. She was sober, stable, and easy to get along with. And she knew the history, so there wouldn't be any illusions. So... why not? I mean, she was my maid of honor, and we spent so much time together again, what did I have to worry about? We got a hotel room one night and did the whole thing. To my surprise, it actually went better than expected. It felt like something fun and casual we could explore without strings. Plus, it felt like we might have someone in our lives we could trust and be open with in that way.

Not long after that, Sam got kicked out of her inpatient treatment facility for fucking around with a male patient. She was on drug court and needed somewhere to live—or she was going to jail. I talked it over with Landon and told her she could stay with us *if* her probation officer approved it. She moved in the next week and settled into a routine:going to work, hitting her meetings, and doing what she was supposed to do. She seemed like she was genuinely trying. Noah loved having her around, and honestly, I appreciated the adult interaction, especially with how tired I was during the final stretch of pregnancy. I wasn't jealous, and I wasn't worried. That kind of drama was behind us— or so I thought.

One night, Landon was drinking in the garage and I was completely exhausted. Pregnancy had been hard on me, with health issues and complications, and I *needed* rest. In the early morning hours, Noah woke up crying, so I brought him upstairs with me and went back to sleep. Landon was passed out drunk on the couch, so I let it be. The next day, I had this weird gut feeling. I asked Landon casually if he had seen Sam after I went to bed. "She came in to bum a smoke," he said, "but I think she went to bed after that." It made sense. I let it go—until Landon started snapping at me during the day. He was crying—no, *bawling*. What the hell was going on?

Snap after snap, he *outed himself... again.* He admitted everything. They kissed in the garage or she kissed him is what he said. They were going to have sex, but before they could make it inside, he started puking. Later, once I'd brought Noah upstairs, instead of turning right and coming up the stairs to his family, to his pregnant wife, he turned left—into the front porch where she was. She gave him a blowjob and he then went back to sleep on the couch like it was any other ordinary morning. He chose that path. And then he lied to me about it.

Lying is the one thing I *absolutely* do not tolerate.

I called her immediately. Of course, she tried to lie. I cut her off: "You have one hour from the time I get home to come get your shit. After that, I'm calling the police for trespassing."

I flew home like a bat out of hell. As soon as I got there, I started hurling her stuff out onto the front lawn—just like in the movies. The hormonal rage was full throttle and there was no going back. When she showed up, she tried to come inside and talk. I met her at the door with my bat in hand.

"Take *one* step closer," I warned her, "and I'm taking you out." Noah had been helping me, and then he said, "Look, auntie, we are playing a game!" I cracked up a little bit between the rage and sent him into the house with Landon. Now was not the time for that.

My heart was shattered. But with my baby coming soon, I didn't have time to break down. I shoved all the feelings deep down and locked them away. Survival mode, full stop. I went on with life like nothing had changed, but everything had. Landon was waiting on me hand and foot, trying to make up for what he did... again. I couldn't care less. I was numb.

2023: No Answer, No Escape

By February, I was 36 weeks pregnant—so close to my due date I could practically feel the baby pressing against time. One morning, I was driving to work like usual. It was early, barely 8 a.m., and the roads were slick. I mean, it was February. I had taken my eyes off the road for ½ a second and looked at my cup holder full of quarters and thought, *Bet I can get a cup of ice!*, I hit a patch of black ice, and before I even knew what was happening, I was upside down in a snowbank. I wasn't wearing a seatbelt, my belly was too big. I held onto the bottom of the steering wheel to keep myself from being thrown around.

Oh my God. Oh my God. What am I going to do?

My legs were wedged in, but I managed to twist free and find my phone. I dialed 911, but the dispatcher kept saying she couldn't hear me.

"You can't hear me? I can't move! What do you mean you can't hear me?"

Panic set in like fire in my veins. I was stranded, pregnant, and terrified. Then—thank God—an electrician who had been driving behind me stopped. He dug through the snow, helped me out, and got me into his truck while we waited for the ambulance. I called Landon. Again. And again. And again. No answer. I kept trying—nothing. I was freaking out. Finally, I called my neighbor, Aria. Even though I still held resentment for what she pulled before the wedding, she was the only one close enough in town who could get to him.

The ambulance finally arrived—and then *it* slid into the ditch, too. *Seriously?!* I started to wonder if I should even get in, but the fire truck came and pulled it out. I climbed in, shaken but stable, and we headed for the hospital. I could feel the wind push us around as we drove through an open field. Landon and my mom were on their way to meet me there. But long story short? He didn't make an appearance that day.

I tried to rest a lot more in the two weeks that followed the crash. I was still pretty shaken up, physically and emotionally. One night, Landon was out in the garage drinking with his buddies. He finally stumbled inside around 1 a.m. This was pretty normal at this time.

I woke up with some mild cramping, but I had been having Braxton Hicks for weeks, so I didn't think much of it. I waddled downstairs to use the bathroom and get a drink of water. When I wiped,there it was: my mucus plug. I wasn't too alarmed. I'd lost it three times during my last pregnancy and still had to be induced, so I figured I had time. But as I lay back down, the cramping didn't stop. It slowly turned into full-blown contractions. I waited about an hour, timing them, breathing through them, and then finally rolled over and shook Landon awake.

"I think we need to go in. I'm having a lot of contractions."

Half-asleep and definitely still drunk, he brushed me off. "Just go back to bed." Now I was mad. I rolled over angrily—and 30 seconds later, *woosh*. My water broke. "No way," I whispered. I rolled back toward him. "We need to go. My water just broke!" He mumbled, "You probably just peed." So I grabbed his hand and stuck it right in the puddle of amniotic fluid. That got his attention. He shot up, wide-eyed. "Alright, let's go."

The drive into town was hell. My contractions were coming fast and hard—it was unbearable. Everything after that moved so quickly it's honestly a blur. At the hospital, my mom held my legs while they tried to place the epidural. The first time, they went too far to the right—which, to this day, permanently messed up my hip and my knee. Once it was finally in place, I laid back and started to relax... and then I started to seize.

I could hear everything, but I couldn't see, move, or speak. I was locked inside myself. They shut the epidural off and waited for me to come back. That was terrifying. They turned it back on again, and within minutes, I was seizing *again*. My mom was holding my face, yelling my name, trying to bring me back. Nothing worked. They ended up giving me *Narcan*—**twice**. That was it—I told them to take the epidural out. Everything after that went fast and hard. I cried, I screamed, "Take this thing out of me, please!!"

Less than an hour later, he was out.

But he wasn't okay.

The First Time I Failed Him

I passed out from the pain. He was blue. It took them a few minutes to get him to cry—but when he did, my heart melted. He had a broken collarbone and had bruises all over his face from being forcefully pulled out of me. My beautiful baby boy—8 pounds, 3 ounces—was sent straight to the NICU.

I got herpes as a teenager, and I ended up giving it to Landon. At 36 weeks pregnant, I was supposed to be on a medication to suppress it, but with everything going on—between the crash, the stress, and the chaos—I never got around to it. After Harlow was born, I noticed he had two small lesions on his chin. Suddenly, infectious disease doctors were in my hospital room. They told me they had to cut the lesions open and send them out for testing. Apparently, you can still have the virus present on your cervix—even if you haven't had an outbreak in a long time. I felt sick. *Did I endanger my baby's life?*

Neonatal herpes can kill a baby. That's why I never let anyone kiss my babies, ever. But that wasn't enough. They wanted Harlow on IV antibiotics for 14 days, and they were planning to do a spinal tap to send samples out of state for more testing. The next 12 days of my baby's life were hell. Even though I was by his side almost every second, I was hurting so deeply—for him and with him. I blamed myself, replaying every what-if in my head. Every time he whimpered or they poked him, it tore me apart. Watching them poke, prod, and inject my newborn was something I wouldn't wish on anyone.

In the end, the tests came back *negative*. No herpes.

The moment they told me, I went into full mama-bear mode. I got us discharged faster than you could blink and let them have it for everything they put my baby through. I chewed their asses for the trauma, the stress, the unnecessary procedures, *all of it.*

High, Low, Lost

For the next year, Harlow was in and out of the hospital, seeing specialists and undergoing two surgeries before we finally found a good rhythm. It drained me completely. I lived in survival mode, running on empty, just trying to make it through each day. As he got older and I was home with him full-time, all the emotions I had stuffed deep down started to rise in ways I couldn't control. I didn't even realize it at first. I was on this sudden high—happy, over-the-top happy. My sex drive skyrocketed, I was spending money without thinking, doing anything and everything just to *feel*. Then came the crash. And it hit at the worst possible time.

Landon was just about to go back to work. He had worked so hard over the years, rising steadily in his company. I should have been proud, supportive—but instead, I unraveled. I was more depressed than I had ever been, and that's saying a lot. I cried constantly, and then one night, I broke.

I told Landon:

"I've been thinking about cheating on you... with Silas."

I hadn't contacted Silas, didn't even know how to. And let's be real—Landon had cheated **three times** already. So just *thinking* about someone else shouldn't have been the end of the world. But it was like I dropped a bomb. We fought for hours that night—yelling, tearing each other down. Every word chipped away at me until I snapped. I went to take a shower. I brought the razor I normally use to shape my eyebrows... and I sliced open my thigh from hip to knee. I wasn't trying to kill myself. I just didn't know how else to get the pain out. I couldn't carry it anymore.

Noah came into the bathroom to talk to me. I thought I moved the curtain fast enough, but the look on his face told me otherwise—he saw. Minutes later, Landon came rushing in. He shut off the shower, pulled me out, and made me get dressed, shaking. He was panicking. He called my mom—even though it was midnight and she lived an hour away. She came. She calmed everyone down. She stayed the night, just in case. That night changed everything. I followed up with my doctor and was finally diagnosed with Bipolar Disorder. It took nearly a year of trying over 20 different medications to find the right balance and keep me regulated. That year was hell, but I got through it. Barley.

Over the next year and a half, things *seemed* like they were moving in the right direction. Sure, there were hiccups here and there, but it felt manageable... until his drinking got worse. It didn't matter what I said or how I begged—the bottle always came first. Eventually, I got used to it. I became, for all intents and purposes, a single mom with someone helping to pay the bills. He went weeks without changing a single diaper. I know he worked hard to provide for us, and I respected that, but... that was all he did. No emotional support. No partnership. No presence.

2024: You Won't Save Yourself - And I'm Done Trying

Even after Landon was diagnosed with stage 3 kidney disease, nothing changed. That year, his kidney function dropped from **50% to 41%**. Our insurance situation was a mess, but beyond that, getting him to a doctor was like dragging a boulder uphill. He wouldn't go unless I forced him. Eventually, I couldn't do it anymore. I told him I wanted out. I couldn't keep carrying the weight of our family alone while watching him self-destruct. I threatened divorce and meant it. For over a month, we were separated under the same roof, alternating who slept on the couch. There was no intimacy, no connection—I gave him all the responsibilities I had been shouldering for years.

I even arranged a surprise intervention—called in everyone who meant something to him. Friends and family traveled from hours away. I thought maybe, just maybe, that would be the wake-up call he needed. It wasn't. He resented me for it, thought I was trying to embarrass or shame him instead of helping him. He shut down and pushed me even further away.

To be honest, I didn't mind the distance.

During that time, I met someone I never expected—someone who made me feel *seen*. Her name was *Chloe*, nine years older than me and going through a nasty divorce herself. We supported each other, laughed over stupid things, and talked like we had known each other for years. She made me feel like a priority, something I hadn't felt in a long time. I told Landon about her—and told him he didn't get a say in what I did anymore.

2025: Magical, Messy, and Gone Too Soon

In January, I made the trip to visit her. It felt like something out of a movie. She took me to a little Mexican restaurant, gave me the cutest Dollar Tree Valentine's gift, and even had her brother give me a tattoo (which... turned out way worse than I expected, but he had just been diagnosed with cancer—I didn't have the heart to complain). That night, as we walked back into the house under the yard light, the snow flurries fell, and Chloe grabbed my hand, spun me around, pulled me close, and kissed me. It was... *magical*. I hadn't felt that in years. But like everything else in my life, it didn't last.

When Landon and I began reconnecting and working through things again, I had to end it with Chloe. I fought with him about it every single day for two months, because I had real feelings for her. Breaking it off broke her and me, and she got petty and shut me out completely. I beat myself up for months afterward, missing what we had, mourning the short time I got to feel like I mattered. But even though I was still torn up inside, things started to get better, quickly.

Landon stepped up. He took charge with the kids—he was present in ways he hadn't been before. We began to do things together as a family that felt genuine, not forced. For the first time in years, it felt like we were actually a team. His drinking? He was sober for almost a month, and even after that, his consumption was down to a third of what it had been before. At first, I was thrown off. I didn't know how to react to the changes. For so long, I had built walls around myself—so high, so impenetrable. I couldn't let myself believe that this was real.

But he genuinely cared—about me, my feelings, and our family. He would take a step back, help me recognize when I was spiraling or just being overly emotional, and gently remind me. He'd do it in such a soft, loving way that it made me want to open up, even though it was hard. He chose me. He chose us. And that was something I never thought I'd see from him. In the past, he would have brushed me off, but now? He stood up for me, for us. He took my side, even when it wasn't easy. He stuck up for me in front of others, which had been a huge issue earlier in our relationship. For the first time, he made it clear—I was his priority. He even got off work early for Noah's first music program—something that would have never happened before.

In so many ways, he grew into the man I needed, the man I had always hoped he would be. He worked so hard to make things right. To make *us* right. And I couldn't believe it, but I had to admit it—I became truly blessed. This wasn't the path I had imagined when we first started out, but somehow, we were here. Together. Stronger than before.

I Am Proof

I used to think survival was the best I could do—just making it to the next day without something breaking, burning, or bleeding. Just trying to breathe without that tightness in my chest. My world was messy, impulsive, and filled with terror. I didn't simply move out and get better. I fought—every single day—dragging myself through it, falling to my knees more times than I can count. But I made my escape. And I made a promise to become everything I never had.

My house isn't always quiet now—but it's loud with laughter. It's filled with love, kindness, and chaos, not anger or vengeance. There's validation here. Consideration. Safety. One night, I caught myself smiling for no reason. No alarms. No drama. Just... love. And in that moment, I realized—for the first time—I wasn't just surviving anymore. I was thriving. We didn't get here clean. We didn't get here easily. But we got here. A place I never thought I'd be.

Now, I'm a mother to my own children. A sister, not a parent, to my siblings. They'll always be my babies, and I'd still do anything for them—but I no longer have to stand between them and the fire every day. I am a wife to a loving husband. A college student on the honor roll, heading into my second degree. Looking back at my high school grades, you'd never think I'd make it here. And I am a friend who can show up without fear.

I am what they could never be.

Author's Note

This memoir is a reflection of my personal experiences and memories, told as accurately as I can recall them. Certain names and identifying details have been changed to protect privacy. Where appropriate, factual details have been supported by public records, including documents from the Minnesota Judicial Branch (publicaccess.courts.state.mn.us). Dialogue and some events have been reconstructed for narrative clarity, but the emotional truth remains intact.

About the Author

Trinity Lease is a writer, wife, mother, and survivor from rural Minnesota. She grew up in a world shaped by chaos, silence, and survival, but found healing in the power of her own voice—and in learning she was never truly alone. Now pursuing her second college degree, Trinity is building the life she once only imagined: one filled with love, safety, and purpose. She lives with her husband and children in a home where laughter echoes louder than the past. This is her first book, written for anyone who's ever felt voiceless, and for those who need to be reminded that survival is just the beginning.

Stay Connected!

Thank you for reading!

If this story spoke to you, I'd love to hear from you! You can connect with me on Facebook @beneath.the.silence.2025, and you can also leave reviews on any platform this book is available (Goodreads, Kindle, Barnes & Noble, Apple Books, Google Books, etc.) in addition to my Facebook page!

If you're interested in having me as a guest on your podcast, YouTube channel, or inviting me to speak at your event, conference, or organization, please don't hesitate to get in touch. I'm passionate about sharing my story in spaces that empower healing, growth, and awareness.

beneaththesilence25@gmail.com

www.ingramcontent.com/pod-product-compliance
Lightning Source LLC
Chambersburg PA
CBHW072347090426
42741CB00012B/2950